Dental Practice Management

Glenys Bridges

About the Author

GLENYS BRIDGES CMIPD, RDN, DIP.DPM

Glenys is an experienced dental practice management and administration trainer with 20 year experience of working with General Dental Practitioners and their teams. In addition she has expertise and qualifications in Counselling and Life Coaching.

She founded an authorised BTEC Edexcel Centre in 1999; she is a Chartered Member of the Institute of Personnel Development.

Glenys began working in training in July 1992; her current activities include training, coaching and business development.

Since 1992, her work has centered on the development of career paths for managers and administrators. She has developed four dentally based BTEC accredited qualifications, ranging in level from 3-5 (NVQ equivalent).

She has also delivered ILM courses as a member of the teaching team at Sandwell College. She has delivered and assessed ILM qualification in First Line Management and Starting Your Own Enterprise.

Her first book *Dental Practice Management and Reception* was published in 2006.

Preface

This book explains contemporary management theories in the context of professional practices and demonstrates how they can be applied as practical techniques to optimise business success. Although written in the context of dental practice management, the theories covered are generic so this book will be a valuable resource for practice managers working in any sector.

Beginning with an explanation of established theories for the development of consistent and measured management skills, readers will be introduced to key theories and case studies to demonstrate the effective and ineffective applications of management techniques.

Glenys Bridges

Published by Stephen Hancocks Limited,
Little Steine, Hill Farm Lane, Duns Tew, OX25 6JH
© Stephen Hancocks Limited 2012.
ISBN 978-0-9565668-1-2

All rights reserved. No part of this publication may be reproduced stored in a retrieval system, or transmitted in any form or by any means electronic, mechanical, photocopying, recording or otherwise, without either the permission of the publisher or a licence permitting restricted copying in the United Kingdom issues by the Copyright Licensing Agency Limited, 90 Tottenham Court Road, London WC1 9HE.

Design and layout by Kavita Graphics, dennis@kavitagraphics.co.uk
Printed and bound by Dennis Barber Limited. Lowestoft, Suffolk

Dental Practice Management

Contents

1. Dental Practice Management 01
2. Understanding your Market and Customers 21
3. Managing Quality Systems 43
4. Systems for Financial Management 57
5. Ongoing Team Development 73
6. Managing Employment Issues 95
7. Promoting a Healthy Workplace 113
   Bibliography and Recommended Reading 132
   Glossary 134
   Index 143

Glenys Bridges

Chapter 1: Dental Practice Management

The role of dental practice manager has evolved over many years. This book aims to provide a range of management tools and techniques for dental managers working in the increasingly regulated primary care environment. This opening chapter provides an overview of the range of skills, models and theories required for effective management. It will define key management terminology and show practical applications for management techniques in the context of day-to-day dental practice management.

Glenys Bridges

Tools and techniques

Small businesses such as dental practices make a substantial contribution to the UK economy. In 2009 the British Chambers of Commerce estimated at 74% of the UK's 15.2 million strong workforce, were employed in 'small businesses'. Small businesses are defined by the number people they employ, with any number between 0 and 100 workers being categorised as a small business.

A significant difference between large corporations and many small businesses is the importance they place upon formal management training and development. Many of the UK's biggest employers such as the NHS and Local Government, place management development programmes at the core of their business strategy, because they recognise that the future success of their operations lies in developing their next generation of managers, providing them with the right mix of knowledge and skills to compete under the existing market conditions. In comparison 74% of workers in small businesses are supervised by managers without any business management expertise.[1]

The need to manage people and operations is frequently viewed as an unwelcome burden for managers in small businesses, who are often so engrossed with day-to-day work tasks that it is difficult for them to find the time for formal management activities. They are not aware that if they were to apply management skills to the preparation and organisation of their business, they would create quality time for their professional and technical work, as illustrated in the fable of the woodcutter, who was felling trees in the forest when a passerby stops, observes him and says,

"You would find your work much easier if you were to stop and sharpen your axe!" The woodcutter, irritated by the stranger's interference replied, "Do you really think I have the time to stop for such luxuries?!!"

All too often managers in small businesses become so caught-up working in the business that they fail to work on the business; that is to plan and prepare so as maximise the return on their input (ROI). Those managers caught up in the day-to-day tasks of working in the business need to set aside time to work on the business. This oversight is sometimes due to a lack of time and/or understanding and is invariably to the long term detriment of the business.

Management theory

Effective management is the product of a good level of knowledge and understanding of the business' economic, legal and interpersonal requirements. It requires application of a range of skills for planning, organising financing as well as people management. Managers of dental services face the same challenges and frustrations as managers in other business sectors. Over the years tried and tested management responses have been developed at the 'sharp end' of business through a process of trial and error. At times these responses have produced brilliant results, yet at other times, results have been disappointing. Academics have determined underpinning management science, through the analysis of management responses and their consequences. This learning has been then used to craft the management theories explored in this book. In each chapter an area of dental practice management will be explored in the context of key management theories in the context of day-to-day operations. This book aims to provide a shortcut to what works in dental businesses.

Management training and education

Over recent years there has been a revolution in dental management education stimulated by the demands arising from the current challenging business environment. Patient requirements and professional regulations have led to concerted pressures on practices to raise their game; and formalise their management. For example, the Care Quality Commission require the practice team to include a registered manager who must supply suitable evidence relating to relevant professional qualifications. There is an ever increasing number of training and qualification options available to enable dental businesses to develop the most appropriate range of management skills to meet the changing demands in dental businesses.

Since 1997 a dentally specific level 4 BTEC management qualification has been available to underpin first line management duties for managers working under the supervision of a more senior, strategic manager. (In most cases this will be a practice principal). Having developed a strong first line management culture, an increasing number of practice managers are now ready to expand their role and, when given the opportunity, purchase shares in a practice and become administrative directors, contributing management input at the boardroom level. In view of this trend the dental management training market has seen a growth in demand for level 5 management qualifications.

To achieve levels 4 and 5 management qualifications requires a huge investment of time and money, from the student and their sponsoring practice. To ensure a satisfactory return on that investment it is vital to choose a qualification at the right level. The National Qualifications and Curriculum Authority issue descriptors of the intellectual skills, processes and accountability each level of qualification characterises. On the basis of these descriptors level 4 qualifications are relevant to those who need to:

- Develop a broad base of management knowledge
- Use a wide range of management skills
- Determine responses to a variety of unpredictable situations, using innovative thinking and a wide range of problem solving skills
- Evaluate information and use the findings for business planning and development.

At this level, management qualifications build underpinning knowledge and ways to apply and evaluate skills covering many areas of management and non- routine activities. Managers are required to provide evidence of appropriate judgment in planning, selecting and presenting information to internal and external customers. For these managers some of their day-to-day work is self-directed and some will be supervised by a senior manager. They will have responsibility for meeting specified quality standards and need a clear understanding of relevant general and dentally specific regulations, plus the ability to apply advanced interpersonal skills to ensure observation of practice policy and protocols. The definition of Level 5 qualifications however are that they aim to enable managers to:

- Generate ideas through the analysis of information and concepts at an abstract level
- Command a wide range of conceptual skills to formulate policy
- Analyse, reformat and evaluate a wide range of information.

These senior management qualifications focus on diagnostic and creative skills. They aim to develop the ability to exercise appropriate judgment for planning and design processes. Level 5 managers are usually responsible for supervising the work of junior managers and accept responsibility for personal and group decisions. They have overall accountability for their designated areas of management.

Defining the management role

Nowadays most practices have an appointed a practice manager. So it is surprising that one of the most frequently asked questions about practice management is 'What do practice managers do?' This is a very basic question and it is crucial that practice management is well defined. The evolutionary path of dental practice management has mirrored that of generic management in that the practice manager role has developed out of administration roles and that good practice, methods and techniques have been established by:

- Experienced managers sharing wisdom gained from hands-on experience
- Social scientists theorising about cause and effect in the workplace.

One of the reasons why the practice manager role is not easily defined is that dental team roles are constantly adapting to meet changing needs. As a result there is no 'one size fits all' definition of dental practice management, resulting in confusion about the management role.

Management theorists

In an attempt to define 'management' it is helpful to refer to Henri Farol's classical definition of management put forward in 1916 as: "To manage is to forecast and plan, to organise, to command, to coordinate and control".

This definition has been expanded upon by contemporary management gurus such as Peter Drucker and Tom Peters, however the essence remains unchanged; and Farol's definition continues to indicate the sort of management input required to underpin successful teams. This very broad definition needs to be tailored to the needs of individual work places. In dental practices an influencing factor will be the extent to which management tasks are delegated and the amount of control the practice owner retains.

In small businesses and professional practices many managers do not hold professional management qualifications. Their qualifications are sector related and they have been selected for a management role because they are a trusted employee. The employer opts to delegate managerial tasks to them, to free-up time to concentrate on income generating work. As a result, when management problems arise, the practice manager may feel overwhelmed and ill-equipped to respond effectively. The difference between qualified and non qualified managers is that qualified managers have learned a range of management techniques, which they can apply to manage situations that arise. Based on Henri Farol's definition, the skills that practice managers need are those required to forecast, plan, organise, command, coordinate and control. A well educated manager knows how to use the following techniques for:

Forecasting

Pest Analysis - Political, Economic, Social, and Technological (PEST) analysis is concerned with the environmental influences on the development and future needs of the business. The acronym stands for the Political, Economic, Social, and Technological issues that could affect the strategic development of a business. This technique explores the macro market in which the business operates, these findings are then assessed using a SWOT analysis to forecast and secure required resources.

Planning

Winston Churchill is credited with the wise words, "Failing to plan is planning to fail". Planning is an important skill for good management with skilful managers maintaining an effective balance between the time spent planning and organising work, with the time spent getting the job done. When the planning process is well structured, similar strategies can be applied in various situations, provided that the plan is kept under review rather than being repeated unquestioningly.

In terms of clinical dental skills, charting is a core patient management activity. The dental chart is a visual map of a patient's dental history and current status used for treatment planning and a constant point of reference for patient care. In terms of management techniques the Gantt chart offers similar benefits for practice management.

The Gantt chart was devised by William Gantt to demonstrate the progress toward the completion of management tasks. Horizontally the chart shows time units and vertically it shows the tasks which are the building blocks of the project. Progress with the tasks is shown with arrows placed at the pre-work stage showing estimated start and finish dates for each task shown in grey. When the task is completed this is changed to blue. In this way the progress of the project is instantly recognisable and it is clear whether the project is running to time or if the plan needs to be reworked to ensure its ultimate timely success.

There are many variation of this chart dependent upon the dimensions of the project (*Figure 1*). This example Gantt chart demonstrates progress for a one-off project, preparation for Care Quality Commission registration. When there is a need for a number of people to participate in an activity, use of a Gantt chart will prevent any part of the activity being overlooked or repeated. For example instead of showing progress with the horizontal arrows, a tick system can be used with team members ticking tasks that have been completed. In this way the manager can instantly assess the status of the activity. It can be used for numerous management projects such as, stock maintenance, x-ray monitoring, staff performance reviews …. the list goes on and on.

Figure 1: An example of a Gantt Chart

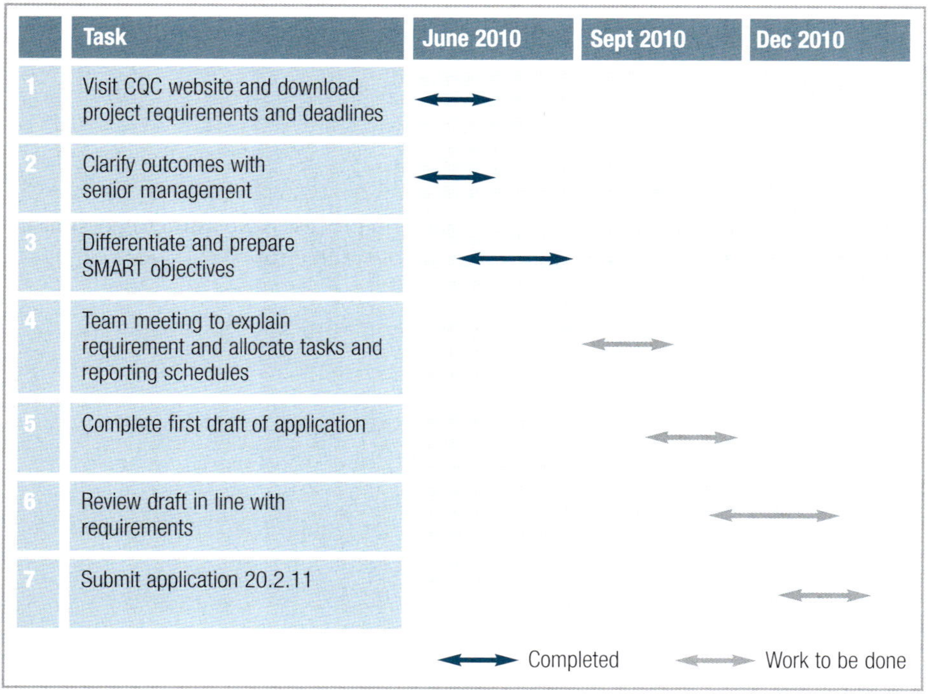

	Task	June 2010	Sept 2010	Dec 2010
1	Visit CQC website and download project requirements and deadlines	←→		
2	Clarify outcomes with senior management	←→		
3	Differentiate and prepare SMART objectives	←——→		
4	Team meeting to explain requirement and allocate tasks and reporting schedules		←→	
5	Complete first draft of application		←→	
6	Review draft in line with requirements			←→
7	Submit application 20.2.11			←→

←——→ Completed   ←--→ Work to be done

There are now a numerous software packages for producing Gantt charts for project planning. Excel is a popular tool for creating Gantt charts, but for more advanced project management activities, tools such as Microsoft Project or a project management add-in for Excel are required. However, if you want to create a simple project schedule and know how to copy/paste/insert/delete in Excel, the Gantt Chart Template shown in *Figure 1* is a MUCH more cost effective solution and easy to use.

The role of practice management is to amalgamate practice activities to optimise time and resources and build a worthwhile practice structure. By definition the role of management is to forecast, and plan, to organise, to command, to coordinate and to control. A series of activities which when followed through skillfully will realise tangible benefits. The development of practice management skills should not be overlooked and it is important that those who aspire to practice management have a good grasp of the established management techniques such as the Gantt chart.

Pareto analysis

Also known as the 80/20 rule, this simple statistical technique can be used to guide decision making based on the premise that 20% of the work produces 80% of the results. The principle is therefore used to ensure you work smarter, rather than working harder. This formal technique is useful to choose between possible courses of action. The manager evaluates the potential costs and benefits of potential actions, and then selects the most effective actions.

Vilfredo Pareto was an Italian economist who noted that approximately 80% of wealth was owned by only 20% of the population. He went on to note that this reflects the lack of symmetry between work put in and results achieved. Pareto analysis is a very simple technique based on the Pareto principle, which is the idea that by doing 20% of work you can generate 80% of the advantage of doing the entire job. Pareto analysis is a formal technique for finding the changes that will give the biggest benefits. Pareto analysis is a simple technique that helps you to prioritise problems and solutions. To use it:

- List the problems and possible solutions
- Group problems and identify causal links
- Score the groups in line with their detrimental effects
- Work on the group with the highest score.

Pareto analysis determines the urgent problems to solve and quantifies the severity of problems.

Mind mapping

This tool is ideal for situations where a group needs to understand all the elements in an issue and is a great tool for brainstorming, issues analysis and planning developed by Tony Buzan in the 1970s. A mind map is a diagram used to represent thoughts, ideas and tasks in words arranged around a central concept. Production of a mind map provides an organised visual overview of a project or idea. Mangers use links to classify information into groupings, branches, or areas with the goal of demonstrating links between portions of information. There are a wide range of free software packages on line to support mind mapping. By presenting ideas in a radial, graphical, non-linear manner, mind maps encourage a brainstorming approach to planning and organisational tasks. Though the branches of mind maps represent hierarchical tree structures, their radial arrangement present the manager with linear visual dimensions and a robust basis for action planning, when ideas are evaluated using the Parato analysis technique.

Commanding

The Elements of Administration are set out by Henri Farol in his code of good governance leading to management success. In the dental sector these are mirrored in the good practice requirements within Clinical Governance.

Coordinating

When the research stages have been completed, the findings can be used to determine SMART objectives. The origins of this technique are disputed however the technique is often accredited to Peter Drucker, as it featured in his book *Management by Objectives* written in 1954, in which he opened up the flood gates to a range of theorists who have introduced their own ideas based on this original concept. Over the years a wide range of interpretations of the SMART acronym have become common place. Numerous attempts have been made to standardise this concept. The most common definition of SMART is 'Specific, Measurable, Achievable, Realistic, and Timed'. However there are other established definitions (*Figure 2*).

Figure 2: Alternative definitions of the acronym SMART

The Dictionary of HR Management 2001	Specific, measurable, agreed, realistic, timed
Human Resource Planning (Vol 29 No 1)	Specific, measurable, attainable, relevant, time-bound
Nursing Management (October 2007)	Specific, measurable, appropriate, realistic, timed
Peter Drucker (The Original version of SMART)	Specific, measurable, achievable, relevant, timed
Updated version	SMART get SMARTER by adding Enjoyable and Recorded

The truth is that:

- There is no definitive version, although S, M and T are usually the same
- The A and R have been played with so much that the terms have become interchangeable
- The A is variously quoted as accurate, agreed, appropriate, attainable, achievable or assignable
- The R is usually realistic or relevant.

The whole point of the acronym is that the terms work together for your enterprise without too much further explanation. If you are using them unthinkingly you are probably failing to identify what you want from them. My preferred version is:

Specific: clear about the task being...
Measurable: the owner can quantify how much of the desired outcome has been achieved
Achievable: the owner believes it is possible to reach the outcome provided that it is
Relevant: the owner believes the outcome is in the scope of their job
Time bound: the outcome needs to be reached within a specific time frame.

Specific objectives are clear and well-defined. They enable the team member to know what is expected of them and the manager to monitor and assess actual performance against the specific objectives.

Measurable objectives are monitored throughout the project and will determine when the work has been completed. They serve to quantify, who is involved, when activities take place, where, how often and can be used to quantify financial aspects.

Achievable; the manager determines what they need to do to ensure the project's success. The consideration being, what is needed to ensure this project is achievable? In this way barriers are recognised and managed. Weaknesses including a lack of skill, under resourcing or manpower shortages and theses can be identified and dealt with. The Achievable analysis ensures that everything is in place for a successful outcome.

Relevant; the consideration is how the success of the project contributes to the mission, philosophy and higher goals as determined in the business plan. Good management is holistic, based on 'joined-up thinking' with all activities being linked to the big picture. In this way it becomes a Gestalt, with the whole being greater than the sum of the parts.

Time bound; objectives should also determine timescales. This may map scheduled completion times for individual stages, as well as when all objectives are due for completion. Timescales should be set to add an appropriate sense of urgency, to ensure momentum and prevent the project ambling over an unreasonably long time span.

Control- quality management

Management control aims to determine consistent results by making the optimum use of practice resources. By setting objectives, allocating manpower and measuring performance the manager is able to make adjustments to counteract shortfalls and establish areas of strength, with an objective of replicating them in areas of underperformance.

In numerous dental practices across the UK, it would be accurate to say that the management is not fit for purpose. In some cases practices consider they have 'tried' practice management and found it did not work for them. In other cases the reluctance to appoint a manager stems from the fact that there are several members of staff who would react adversely, should any particular colleague be promoted and become their manager. In some cases where the practice management initiative has failed, the root cause has been a lack of support for a newly appointed manager, whether this is because they are a manager from another work sector, employed to bring management skills into the dental team, or an existing team member favoured with promotion to be the practice manager.

When attempts to establish a formal practice management role fail, it is often because the management model that has been selected is incompatible with the needs of the business and the team. There are numerous management models each featuring different roles and responsibilities and relying on different team interactions. The right model for any given practice will be determined by the size, philosophy, and history of the practice. Irrespective of the management model chosen, successful management relies on practice owners providing a strategic framework as the foundation for the work of the practice manager. The two most popular management models for dental teams are as follows:

The co-operative model

Some practices prefer to avoid hierarchical structures. They favour a management based on peer or collective decision making. In this model, management responsibilities are shared and decision-making is normally by consensus, with no individual having authority to manage the work of the others. The practice therefore creates a managing body composed of each team member. This approach is seen by its advocates as being the most democratic management style. However, it is without doubt the most difficult model to maintain, because it requires:

- A shared sense of purpose
- Exceptional levels of commitment from everyone
- Willingness to accept responsibility for others' work
- The ability to make decisions by consensus.

When this model works well, the practice benefits from the direct involvement of front-line workers in decision-making, synergy and the camaraderie this generates. There are however a couple of primary areas of concern with the co-operative model, one being that compromise is an essential for success, but at times ideological or philosophical differences will obstruct compromise. The other being that consistent reporting and accountability structures are difficult to maintain in the collective model. There is no effective way to ensure that accountability for individual actions is maintained.

Management team model

This is used in many successful practices. It is based on the formation of a management team and democratic workplace structures. Many management books and articles written since the 1970s advocate this model. Practices operating under the Management Team Model are characterised by a high degree of team involvement in operational and administrative activities, under the supervision of a professional manager. Here the role of the manager is to offer directive supervision. Structurally, there may be many groups and subgroups with some decision-making authority. Their decision-making extends to defining operational details of strategic policy, by determining the practical aspects of procedure and administrative processes.

This model works best when managers have been selected for their knowledge, skills, attitude, aptitude and experience. The most important shortcoming of this approach is that it can provide scope for micro-management if the manager fails to delegate authority, believing that their role requires them to make all operational decisions, leaving only the implementation for the team, who feel undermined and lose engagement. Changing a management model is like changing a lifestyle, it involves abandoning comfortable habits and replacing them with unfamiliar roles and activities. Should you choose to change your management model the transitional difficulties cannot be overstated. To accomplish this type of change requires focus, time, and energy. In addition everyone affected must consider there will be adequate payback for their efforts.

The business plan

The reasons given by practice managers for not producing a formal business plan is that the example business plans available for guidance purposes are very complex and simply seem to be a way to make work for those who do not have enough to do. In actual fact, the time and energy spent writing a business plan setting aims and objectives, is an excellent investment in the business. A high quality business plan is a crucial business tool which provides:

- A reference point for decision making
- Standards to identify and manage underperformance
- Clarification of practice philosophy for the guidance of policy and procedures
- Benchmarks for job descriptions and appraisals
- Rationale for services offered, practice development and marketing
- Figures to calculate treatment fees.

Without a formal business plan, management can only be reactive which is tantamount to gambling away your own financial security and that of your staff and suppliers. Creating a business plan is the first vital step to proactive practice management. A good business plan gives the business focus and a sound basis upon which to make business decisions. Before any management model can add value to the business, senior managers must create the business plan which is the practice manager's mandate for action, as all actions and activities should be formulated to secure targets and objectives set out in the plan.

Before 2008 few people outside of the financial sector realised that severe financial downturn was imminent. Since the onset of the financial downturn even the best planned businesses have needed to revisit and revise their plans. In doing so, they are consciously making decisions to drive their way through, rather than being derailed by the resulting changes in the business environment. Even if you have never produced a formal business plan before, it would be reckless to proceed without one now. When writing a business plan open with a formal description of your business in which you:

- Explain the business's goals and philosophy
- Identify its products and services
- Describe the profile of the people who purchase and provide goods and services
- Set goals for service and profitability.

Close with historical information about how and why the practice was formed, and how the business goals can be achieved.

An important objective of the plan is to ensure that everyone is aware of the business's direction and are committed to achieving its goals. The plan does not need to be complex or wordy, it simply needs to communicate the business's direction and provide the team with reference points for decision-making.

Dental Practice Management

The business plan summaries the business vision over 1, 3 and 5 years, which should then be the basis for policy development and determining future direction of the business. It is a communication tool with which you can ensure those who have a part to play in securing the business's goals can see the bigger picture and recognise their role in the success of the business.

In many cases there are two versions of the business plan in existence, the full version which includes confidential financial information, and a shorter version showing generalised income and expenditure for general distribution throughout the team. Some practices publish this version on their website. There is no one set format for a business plan, the content typically includes:

- Cover page: identifying the business image and strap line
- Table of contents: to organise the information for the reader
- Business profile: stating skills and qualifications within the business
- Executive summary: providing the 'big picture', stating aims and objectives for 1, 3 and 5 years in the context of your market, highlighting the factors that will lead to success
- Marketing plan: an outline of your marketing strategy
- Operations: a summary of how services will be created and delivered
- Financial statements: financial performance based on the plan's assumptions
- Appendix: including statistical analyses, marketing materials, and résumés.

Good business plans are dynamic, written and rewritten in response to internal and external influences upon the business.

The cover page

Make this page the shop window for your business, let it convey the practice's personality and give the reader a feeling for its ethos. Many businesses adopt a strap line, this is sentence used to emphasise the essence of the practice, for example 'our aim is to care'. The strapline promotes your brand and draws attention to the fundamental nature of the practice. It is displayed on headed note paper, the practice website and all patient literature.

Table of contents

To direct the reader to key information.

Business profile

This provides a comprehensive picture of your practice, including:

Formal details:
- The length of time it has been established
- Type of work carried out at your practice
- Geographical and patient demographics
- A business structure diagram
- Details of the business ownership.

An explanation of what you will do to:
- Distinguish your practice
- Ensure patients benefit through buying your products and services
- Develop services to meet customers' changing needs.

It is important to cover any challenges you feel the business may face to show how you plan to manage them. Explain key features of the dental business such as special regulations, technology requirements and patient expectations.

Executive summary

The executive summary outlines your whole business. Although it is not shown at the front of the plan it is the guiding principles of the plan. This is often where you begin when writing a business plan; it is where you identify aims and objectives for the span of the plan. You will not be able to complete this section until you have completed the other sections of the business plan.

The executive summary highlights the most important points:

- Goals, targets and practice philosophy
- Opportunity in the market
- Management team
- Track record to date
- Financial projections
- Funding requirements and expected returns.

Dental Practice Management

Marketing plan

The time spent researching the market and planning service delivery will be rewarded with the production of an accurate projection of the business's chances of success. Begin with an analysis of how your services will meet your customers' specific needs, then go on to show how you will position your product in terms of price, quality, response time and after-sales service compared with competitors.

Estimate the minimum amount of business you need to secure break-even, and then consider how you will attract that business. Show how long you predict each sale will take. Many businesses introducing new products or treatments underestimate the time involved in winning and delivering each treatment.

Identify who your customers are. Show the finding of your research into which existing patients have expressed an interest in, or promised to buy from you; and the sales they represent. State how you will identify potential new patients. Unless you can demonstrate that you have a clearly defined pool of potential new patients business development is likely to be a struggle. Specify how will you promote your product e.g. using advertising, PR, direct mail, email or through your website.

Operations

In this section show exactly how you will use the resources available to you to run the business and explain what facilities the business has and how it will deliver dental care to patients.

- State the pros and cons of the practice location
- Indicate the facilities you have /need, equipment and machinery
- Consider any potential limits to production capacity
- Provide a list of employee roles you need to fill and the skills required to fill them
- Show how you selected your suppliers.

Financial statements and projections

There is no point in spending hours producing detailed financial forecasts if you are not going to use them to control the business. Each aspect of financial management should be well researched. The accounting world has a language of its own, which can seem impenetrable to those of us who have not spent years studying its intricacies. Nevertheless, solid financial rationale should underpin all business decisions, so it is essential to become financially literate. This begins with learning how to read the practice accounts and pick up trends and the implementations of decisions made over the financial period. There are four financial reports that you need to be able to read in connection with each other these are:

Profit and loss accounts

Also known as the income statement, P&L accounts show the income received from the sale of goods and services and the all important costs of sales; how much you have spent to generate this income. This includes staff wages, materials and overheads. The role of the manager is to ensure the percentage increase in costs is less than the percentage increase in revenue, in which case you have controlled your direct cost base.

The aim is to calculate the all important operating profit, which is money earned from your business activities after deducting direct cost of sales and indirect expenses; this shows profitability.

Balance sheets

This gives the practice's financial position at a specified point in time: It shows the total value of the net financial and material assets (what you own), less liabilities (what you owe). There is often debate about how these figures are calculated. Traditionally the price paid for goods has been used in this calculation. In the current financial climate it can be more provident to use the market value of purchases at a given time to prevent assets from being over valued and so making the balance sheet meaningless. When all liabilities have been settled, the remaining value of the practice's assets is known as equity.

Cash flow statement

This is a most important working document that practice managers need to use on a day-to-day basis for decision making. It tracks the actual movement of cash into and out of a business over a financial period. This is in contrast to the profit and loss, which records income when it is earned and expenses when they are due for payment, whether or not the cash has been received/paid. It is not unknown for businesses with a healthy P&L to go under because the money they need to settle with their creditors is not immediately available, although it has been earned but not paid to the business.

Notes to accounts

Practice managers need to be able to interpret the information provided by the financial documents discussed above. They also need to be able to read between the lines of the annual account, produced by the practice accountants. Annual accounts will be supplemented by Notes to the accounts. These notes provided background information, such as how decisions on the value of assets have been reached. Many company owners read financial statements from back to front, in this way they can understand the underpinning judgments before looking at actual results.

Each of these financial statements needs to be considered in conjunction with each other, to give an insight of the financial health of the practice. You need understanding of each of these statements. When compared with statements from prior periods, you can determine whether something is happening in your business that needs your special attention. Your accountant can prepare these statements for you from the business data that you supply. There are also a number of computer software programs that will help you generate these statements from your input of regular transactions, such as sales, collections, purchases, payments and payroll.

Appendices

These may include detailed financial forecasts (monthly sales, monthly cash flow, P&L). For example, the profit margin on each product, debtor collection period, creditor payment period, stock turn over, interest and equipment purchases.

You may also want to include:

- Detailed CVs of key personnel
- Market research data
- Practice Information Leaflet
- A list of external data sources used in your research will add credibility to the information.

Business plans are as individual as the businesses they detail. They offer managers the opportunities to consider and forecast future performance, so pitfalls can be avoided.

Chapter 2:
Understanding your Market and Customers

Long term business success is built upon customer centred business strategies that are responsive to customers' wants and needs. It is only by focusing on their purchasers and providers, that managers are able to develop the goods and services their customers will buy.

There are a range of theories and techniques widely used to research, design, plan and deliver profitable services. The techniques covered in this chapter are:

- PESTLE analysis
- The Marketing Mix
- Porters Five Forces Model
- SWOT Analysis
- The Operational Management Process
- Critical Analysis.

By using a combination of these techniques managers can assess current customer and market trends and so determine how effectively to promote services to target customer groups. The aim of marketing is to ensure that the needs of *internal* and *external* customers are fully recognised and met. This begins with effective market research and the skilful interpretation of findings. Success in marketing requires a good grasp of customer psychology, to secure a good understanding of how emotional and financial factors affect purchasing behaviour. Market research should observe customer rights and the cultural, ethical and environmental standards set by the dental profession.

Marketing

The Chartered Institute of Marketing defines marketing as: *The management process responsible for identifying, anticipating and satisfying customer requirements, profitably.*

Analysis of this definition reveals that the cornerstone of marketing is a clear understanding of any market forces and factors affecting the business, so that the business can optimise all resulting benefits and avoid any associated drawbacks. Managing marketing activities starts with the development of a marketing plan based upon the business plan, in which the practice philosophy, vision, objectives and targets are established. The marketing plan defines operational measures to respond to the established needs of the external customers who purchase dental care and so provide the business's income. It also accounts for the needs of the internal customers who deliver the dental services that patients purchase.

Dental Practice Management

The techniques
Market research

When conducting marketing initiatives businesses expect to invest money, time, or resources and to secure a return on their investment. In financial terms, rate of return (ROR), also known as return on investment (ROI), is the ratio of money gained or lost on an investment, relative to the amount of money, time or resources invested.

In conducting market research the manager aims to project the potential benefits given marketing activities can realise for the business. This could be measured in terms of:

- Increased sales
- Better patient retention
- Raised public profile
- Increased referrals
- Reduction in missed appointments
- Better team morale.

The manager must also project the cost of bringing services to the market, so they are able to determine a pricing structure to cover those costs. When these calculations are made at an early stage the decision not to proceed on a potentially unprofitable project can be made to prevent the business losing money.

Market research can be used to:

- Explore the possibilities of a new marketing idea
- Determine the most effective way to increase turnover.

When the aim of your research is to find supporting evidence for a preferred course of action it is essential to be aware that your research may indicate that an alternative course of action would be more productive.

A valuable management technique for producing a marketing plan is the seven stages Operational Management Process. This technique relies on a firm understanding of the *Macro Market*, and the *Micro Market* operating within the practice.

Skills and activities of the Operational Management Process

The operational management process is a structured, logical and methodical management technique that enables managers to take a considered approach to management initiatives. It is an eclectic approach derived from the work of theorists such as Farol, Brech and Peters. The technique uses a staged approach, breaking down the activities at each stage into an audit trail for final assessment of the success and value of the results. In marketing as in any other area of management a considered and structured approach is the key to success. The technique consists of the following stages:

- **Initiation** - This is a trigger setting a course of events into motion. Proactive management initiatives are triggered when managers consider the needs the initiative must meet and select appropriate research measures. In some cases the manager must adopt a reactive response, for example, when new legislation is introduced and the manager needs to design compliance measures. Initiation is the point at which managers recognise the need to act.

- **Research** – This is a systematic investigation of the facts, conducted before taking action to ensure that you do not blunder in blindly. At this point the manager assesses the resources available and begins to visualise the end result. As advocated by Steven Covey in his book *The Seven Habits of Highly Effective People* in which he states that highly effective people 'begin with the end in mind'. Through a process of questioning and consideration of the information gathered, they increase their understanding of how to achieve their strategic objectives.

- **Design** – Here the project's framework (what needs to be done) is identified. At the design stage the manager creates the strategy, preparing the way for the tactical planning stage, when the practicalities of HOW to proceed are made. The design needs to be detailed and specific; the term 'To be terrific you must be specific', highlights the importance of SMART objectives at the design stage which can be audited and evaluated at the appropriate time. With SMART objectives in place it is possible to create a detailed action plan.

- **Planning** – Is the act of formulating a programme for a definite course of action. At this stage the manager decides how to achieve the end result and allocates resources. Here practicalities are agreed e.g. a list of the actions required are inserted into an action plan and linked to a time measured programme to complete the project on schedule, progressing the project from a concept to reality.

- **Implementation** - The process of putting the plan into action. It is important to keep a record of events for analysis, noting all aspects where expectations were either exceeded or unattained. Recording this for later analysis will enable the definition of best practice for future activities.

- **Audit** – This is a review and examination of objective information (facts and figures) to test the adequacy and effectiveness of progress towards specific objectives. This will take place when the Time Measured aspect of the SMART objectives has elapsed, when the manager refers back to the objectives specified at the design stage.

- **Evaluation** – In this context the evaluation is essentially a set of philosophies and techniques to determine how well the results contribute to the overall targets of the practice set in the business plan.

PESTLE analysis

This technique is used to determine any **P**olitical, **E**conomic, **S**ociological, **T**echnological, **L**egal or **E**nvironmental aspects which will enhance or undermine your project. When your research is complete you will need to evaluate the PESTLE elements with a SWOT analysis to calculate how these will potentially impact on the success of your marketing project.

PESTLE Analysis will help you to:

- Define the kind of people you want to reach by age, lifestyle and social status. Once you have your patient profile you can find out what they read and where they go. Then consider a range of ways to get your message to them.
- Encourage repeat orders. People who have bought from you once are likely to do so again. Keep scrupulous records of your customers and give them top priority in all your mail-shots and marketing campaigns. Thank them for their loyalty and offer small gifts - increasing in value as their orders stack up.

Marketing is a science, and necessitates trial and error, but the effectiveness of any particular project must be audited and critically analysed. This requires careful monitoring which should take place at the designated time preset in the *Time Measured* aspect of the SMART objectives. It is essential to allow enough time for the project's potential to be realised, don't be too hasty in your conclusions - sometimes there's a 'slow burn' factor. Interested parties may need time to reach a purchasing decision.

PESTLE in **practice**

PESTLE analysis is used to make strategic decisions concerned with:

- Matching activities to the macro environment
- Scope of the practice activities – what it does or does not do
- Matching activities to available resources
- Allocation of resources and technology
- Long term business direction
- Implications for change across the whole organisation.

These decisions are made with regard to:

- **POLITICAL**: Global, national, regional, local and community trends, changes, events etc
- **ECONOMIC**: World, national and local trends, changes, events etc
- **SOCIAL**: Developments in society – culture, behaviours, expectations
- **TECHNOLOGICAL**: Developments including computer hardware, software, applications, other equipment, materials, products and processes etc
- **LEGAL**: World/EU/National legislation changes, prospects etc
- **ENVIRONMENTAL**: Global/EU/National /local issues, pressures, movements etc.

Taking the above factors into account a PESTLE analysis framework can be produced (*Figure 1*).

Figure 1: An example of a PESTLE analysis

EXTERNAL FACTORS	1. Factors	2. Implications	3. Relative importance of implications			
			Time	Type	Dynamics	Relative Importance
POLITICAL	VAT Rising	Materials costing more	Now	Negative	>	Critical
ECONOMIC	Increase in Minimum Wage	Salary increase	Now and future	Negative	>	Critical
	National budget deficit	Local unemployment high				
	Interest free credit	Employed pts can spread cost of top end procedures		Positive		
SOCIAL	Safety	Health & Safety legislation	Now and future	Negative	>	Important
	Media Image	People want to Look younger		Positive		
TECHNOLOGICAL	New software introduced	Speed some processes up	Now	Positive	>	Very Important
	Photoshop enhancement	Patients can see before they buy		Positive		
LEGAL	Legislation changes	Import/Export changes	Future	Could be either	>	Very Important
	Care Quality Commission registration	Can demonstrate quality measures	Now	Positive		Very Important
ENVIRONMENTAL	Green initiatives	New working practices	Now	Positive	>	Important

Having used a PESTLE analysis to define the Macro environment, you can SWOT analyse to establish whether the elements can be perceived as a strength, weakness, opportunity or threat

Michael E Porter's Five Forces of Competitive Position model

Michael Porter, a professor at Harvard Business School, has developed a Five Forces of Competitive Position model to take a detailed look at aspects of competitive strength and the position of your business in the local market. The value of this model is that it enables managers to represent complex concepts in relatively easily accessible format. The Five Forces model analyses market factors to enable managers to make a strategic assessment of their competitive position in a given market. The five forces that Porter suggests drive competition are:

1. Existing competitive rivalry between suppliers
2. Threat of new market entrants
3. Bargaining power of buyers
4. Power of suppliers
5. Threat of substitute products (including technology change).

The Micro market

Marketing Mix is a poplar technique when defining the businesses *Micro* market. The most successful businesses are built around their customers' requirements. By focusing on customers they increase their chances of competitive success, by designing business activities based upon analysis of the elements of the marketing mix, making marketing decisions to create 'best fit' solutions to meet the recognised needs and wants of both the internal customers (the dental team-providers of services) and the external customers (the patients- purchasers of dental services). When this balance is right it will influence customers' perceptions of the practice and therefore their motivation and purchasing behaviour. The marketing mix theory was first introduced in 1953 by Neil Borden, in his presidential address to the American Marketing Association when he first coined the term. Prominent marketer, E. Jerome McCarthy, proposed the 4 P classifications in 1960, which has seen numerous variations on the

Dental Practice Management

theme dependant upon sector requirements. The 5Ps are widely used in the dental sector:

- Product
- Price
- Promotion
- Place
- People.

The marketing mix in practice

Price – is a critical element of the mix which can easily become a deal breaker. Customers will always look for value for money. The challenge for marketing managers is to convince their customer that the features and benefits of the product provide that value for money. It is widely considered that customers buy the *benefits* derived from their purchases, whilst the features of the purchase will influence the decision as to which product to buy.

- **Features** of treatments are the specs of a treatment which may include convenient appointments, time in the chair, interest free finance available
- **Benefits** of treatments may be to eat speak and smile with confidence.

Patient education is vital in respect of the price aspect, as it has the potential to shift the customer's focus from the price, to the value of treatment.

Cost of sales – when pricing services and treatments it is vital to calculate the cost of sales to ensure the price is viable. When businesses price goods and services to beat their competitors on price, they risk under pricing and financial ruin.

Promotion – promotional aspects are wide and varied and include any aspect that affects the practice image. It includes the obvious features such as advertising, direct marketing, packaging, personal selling, public relations and sales promotion.

To identify optimal promotional activities reference should be made to the findings of the PESTLE and SWOT analysis, to match the promotional activities to the market. It goes without saying that when you are selling top end private dentistry you need a different approach than you would to attract patients for NHS care, because what attracts some groups of customers would deter others, you need to understand the people you want to attract and cater for their preferences.

Advertising to raise awareness and promote services can be very costly unless you make use of a range of ways to advertise free of charge. There are plenty of places to get your practice mentioned for nothing, such as the free listings of Yellow Pages, Thompson Directory, the BT Phone and other consumer information guides. There are an increasing number of web directories now which carry free listings, and your local Chamber of Commerce booklets. On the old-fashioned side of things, stick your leaflets up on any free notice boards in libraries, halls, and community centres, medical practices and staff rooms.

The media can be an important a source of free publicity that can give an enormous boost. New products or features in the national, even local paper can bring in millions. A quarter page advertisement in the nationals would cost thousands - the equivalent in editorial space is free of charge! You can email details to the editorial desk of your chosen publication and take it from there.

Keep your website up-to-date; ensure you include details of all existing and evolving products and services. Be aware that the key words you use will become 'key words' for web search engines, so make sure you use all the words in your site that your patients will use when searching for dental services.

Word of mouth is a primary source of new patients, so give it a helping hand, by giving patients a simple referral form and offering them incentives to introduce a friend to your products. People like to know about how your existing patients feel about the practice, so put thank you letters and other positive publicity in your brochures and on the practice website.

Being high profile in the local community is an excellent way to attract attention. Being a sponsor can often yield big publicity for a modest investment. Typical examples are amateur or professional football clubs (you can pay for the kit and put your name on the shirts), arts organisations, community groups and charity fundraising events.

Place – the features of your practice premises are an important part of this aspect of the marketing mix, as too is the availability of car parking or public transport. The business plan should determine the profile of the patients you want to attract. If you are aiming to be a family practice, including child friendly aspects of the practice will make you attractive to families, whereas if you are located in an area with large numbers of industrial or commercial units you may want to make adults the focus of your patient base. Decisions about the features of your premises should be made with consideration of the people directly or indirectly involved in the delivery and consumption of your product, including the dental team. Their interactions can influence the perceived value of your product and organisation.

Product – when considering your product, rather than focusing on the features of treatments, look at the benefits you are selling to your patients, as this is what they want. Make sure the product is presented in ways that best show you have understood your patient's requirements and design services to satisfy customer and consumer needs now and continually fine-tune and dynamically modify them to accommodate changing needs and market conditions.

Listening to customers

When the only feedback gathered about how internal and external customers experience your practice is when a complaint is made, you are not running a customer-centred practice. To get a holistic insight into how customers experience the practice you need to actively gather the range of information covered through the 3Cs:

- Comments
- Complaints
- Compliments.

The 3Cs technique in practice

This technique should be used to explore the extent to which the needs of internal and external customers are being met. Businesses should aim to meet the needs of the customers who purchase their goods and services, however to achieve this in the long term they need to meet the needs of the internal customers providing those services. The purpose of this approach is to create a happy balance between the needs of both customer groups.

Comments
External customers – as dental professionals our attitude towards dental services is different to those of our patients, for whom dentistry is a much smaller part of their lives, than it is of ours. We cannot even begin to see dentistry in the same way and so

we need to find ways of gathering information that will enable us to see the practice through their eyes. In this way we can identify their needs and then use our knowledge of dentistry and dental services to meet those needs.

There are a range of ways we can gather comments, all of which have their specific value and recovering requirements. It is always a good idea to invite comments face to face from patients, as well as giving them the chance to give less favourable feedback without putting themselves on the spot. An anonymous questionnaire is helpful so long as it is distributed consistently and not only when you expect a glowing reply.

Even comments about the practice colour scheme or the books in the waiting room are an important insight into how patients see the practice. If we listen carefully to our patients they will tell us what they need and we can design our services around those needs.

Internal Customers – comments and feedback from the team should be encouraged on an ongoing basis. An increasing number of teams have introduced a morning 'huggle', in which they share relevant information about the day ahead. It is a mistake to let matters escalate and become problematic, when by having an early discussion the matter can be brought to a timely resolution.

Complaints
External customers – complaint handling skills are a core CPD element for General Dental Council (GDC) registrants. A complaint handled well can improve your relationship with the complainant. For the dental professional, when the customer's problems are handled well at an early stage, formal complaints can be avoided. Sometimes you will lose a customer if the relationship has broken down completely. However, most situations can be resolved by taking appropriate action as soon as the problem becomes evident. An in-house complaints procedure was introduced into dental practices from April 1996 and updated in April 2000. The GDC developed the required measures following the recommendations of the Wilson Report.

Most dental patients who are unhappy about any aspect of their dental care do not complain. They may go elsewhere and tell others why they have left you, which is detrimental for your practice image and may prevent you from attracting new patients. Therefore, an efficient, user-friendly complaints handling system can benefit your practice.

Dental Practice Management

Internal customers – unfortunately in some teams grumbling can become a way of life. When this happens the energy levels of the team are depleted and it becomes difficult to motivate staff to adopt new working practices.

The practice grievance procedure should work for the team in the same way as the complaints scheme does for patients. It encourages grievances to be specific and for a process of discussion and negotiation to take place to find a win-win solution in much the same way.

Compliments

External customers – when patients are delighted with the services and the products they receive from us we need to take careful note of exactly what it was about their experiences of the practice that met and exceeded their expectations. When we know what we are doing right we can do more of it.

Sometimes when a patient is delighted by our services, it is because an individual member of staff has 'Gone the Extra Mile' for them. The service culture in the dental team is important and should be built into our procedures rather than being based on an element of chance. Here, service standards can be set and enforced to ensure a consistent level of patient care.

Good communication is a balance of giving and receiving information. When planning and building services for patients we must involve them at every stage to ensure that we are striking a balance between meeting the needs of both the purchasers and providers of dental services.

Internal customers – the biggest compliment your internal customers can give the practice is to continue to contribute their best efforts toward the achievement of the practice's objectives. When people understand their role in the success of the practice and can see the progress being made they will compliment the practice in all they say and do.

SWOT analysis

Having completed the market research a SWOT analysis can be used to interpret the findings. The origins and a definitive description of this widely recognised contemporised management technique are vague and highly contended. Where the SWOT technique originated, be it from Harvard professors or Stanford scholars, is irrelevant. It is more important to note that this technique has been used in various formats for more than 50 years, which is evidence of its universal appeal for assessing viability, resources and the business environment.

SWOT analysis in practice

This is a staged evaluative process to predict or conduct a post-project evaluation of an activity or process. The first stage is to identify strengths and weaknesses, then go on to specify any opportunities or threats arising from those strengths and weaknesses.

- **Step 1**: Identify the most positive aspects of the process or activity: these are the strengths
- **Step 2**: Identify any weaknesses of the process or activity: these are the weaknesses
- **Step 3**: Identify any opportunities arising from the strengths and weaknesses
- **Step 4**: Identify any threats arising from strengths and weaknesses

SWOT in Practice

STRENGTHS	WEAKNESSES
• Interest free credit is available for some patients • Local area not too badly affected by financial downturn • We have a good health and safety record • We have state of the art software including a patient education package • We have a good rapport and a long term relationship with the majority of our patients	• No time or private space to explain finance options • Large number of patients in minimum wage work • VAT increase in Jan 2011 • No time to show patients education software and communicate the value of procedures • Many of our established patients do not know what services are available at the practice
OPPORTUNITIES	**THREATS**
• To develop a team role for explaining patients treatment options and promoting • To promote the practice on the basis of health and safety measures • To promote features and benefits of advanced procedures • An email marketing campaign could update existing patients on the range of treatments and finance options	• Some dentists may not want to hand over treatment coordination activities • VAT increase will increase practice running costs, patient charges will need to be increased to cover this • Patients raise queries about procedure with reception staff

Dental Practice Management

Summary of findings and recommendations

There is a potential to maintain a high level of private income. We will need to develop a treatment coordination programme to ensure that all patients are aware of the range of treatments we offer and the payment schemes available to spread the cost of treatment.

We will need to train trusted senior nurses as treatment coordinators to ensure the service is available at all times.

Project design

Having completed market reach and analysed the findings you are ready to develop the project's strategy in SMART objectives. (see Chapter 1): Based on the practical example covered in this chapter they could read as follows:

SPECIFIC	• Initiate a care coordination programme to introduce new patients to the practice philosophy and the range of treatments offered
MEASURABLE	• All new patients will be seen by a treatment coordinator for 10 mins before their initial clinical assessment • Following the assessment the care coordinator will explain treatment options and use the software package to show patients the value of treatments, so they can make fully informed choices • The care coordinator will explain our terms and conditions of treatment to patients • A budget of £1,000 for capital expenditure will be awarded • Email marketing campaign consisting of a series of four messages will go to existing patients to encourage enquires about new treatments
ACHIEVABLE	• This will require the management to define the systems and place two senior nurses on a treatment coordination course • Records of treatment uptake following treatment coordination must be kept to justify expenditure of wages for care coordination • A care coordination suite must available • Reception staff must be on board and clear about systems for booking in patients
RELEVANT	• Unless our patients are aware of the aesthetic treatments we offer and how they can be financed they will not buy them
TIME MEASURED	• The results will be assessed and patient questionnaires completed after a series of four email shots has been sent to existing patients Allowing preparation time, the results will be audited after eight weeks

Customer care strategy

In dentistry, the short term value lies in delighting patients with transformational treatments and the long term value in prevention; in both cases the most effective way to raise the perception of value lies in customer care activities.

High standards of customer care are embedded in the philosophical and ethical culture of dentistry. Standards for patient care are outlined in *Standards for Dental Professionals*, issued by the GDC and available on their website (www.gdc-uk.org). These standards address aspects of both customer and clinical care. Practices need to translate the standards into practical service standards to look after patients and ensure their wants, needs and expectations are met and exceeded, thus creating customer satisfaction and loyalty. This means looking at everything the practice does when providing services to patients; and finding ways to give patients something of value that they did not expect.

To prevent customer care measures from losing their edge they should be regularly measured and monitored from the patients' and the practice's points of view. It is a good idea for this review to be the responsibility of the front of house team, with ongoing processes to determine details of how services are delivered. The ideal starting point for such a review process is to go back to basics and re-establish the practice's strategy and philosophy for customer care.

Customer care strategy should be discussed by the team, so everyone is aware of the practice's intentions, customer orientation and the part each person is expected to play. To make realistic decisions about how to offer the most effective customer care the team needs agreed service standards and methods for assessing the extent to which they are being achieved. This in turn needs well considered training and communication channels in place to ensure the consistent delivery of measures and a range of ways to recognise and reward teams and individuals for good performance. The essence of a good strategy is how it transforms 'problem' behaviour to 'the desired' behaviour.

On a practical level the aims of customer care measures are simply to:

- Managing all customer contact to mutual benefit
- Promote patients' loyalty to the practice.

With a clear vision of the results you want to achieve, the next step is to measure and monitor the extent to which you are achieving those standards so that corrective action can be taken if and when required.

Service standards are the measurable part of your customer care strategy and will fall into several categories such as:

- Waiting times at and for appointments
- The extent to which patients' expectations have been met in service delivery
- The extent to which patients are informed and able to make informed choices between treatment options
- Communication about terms of business and payment requirements
- The speed of response to requests, enquires, complaints or services
- The quality of response to requests, enquires, complaints or services
- The extent to which a consistently friendly/professional approach is extended to all patients at all times by the entire dental team.

The most frequently used methods to measure and maintain customer care activities are questionnaires, customer surveys, mystery shopping and benchmarking. Once information from these methods is collected it is essential there is a follow-through and the results are used in high profile ways to support decision-making and ongoing training to ensure continuous improvements.

Although a genuine concern for the happiness and well being of patients is the life blood of value of quality customer care, I have worked with many practices to ensure that customer care is not a random approach dependant upon people and circumstances, and to introduce a managed approach and agreed services standards for the entire team.

Planning in practice

By using a Gantt chart to plan you project (see Chapter 1) you will be able to allocate team roles throughout the work team. This requires you to give each person clear goals and targets. They also need clear reporting procedures so that you can monitor progress without the need to micromanage delegated work. Such details will originate from the SMART objectives and the business plan which supports the purpose of any business to create wealth by providing goods or services, i.e. to make a sufficient profit from its activities to provide a living for the team and enough money to reinvest in business development.

At the planning stage a budget must be set which will quantify your target for return on investment. In most cases this will be calculated in terms of best, middle and worst case scenarios.

Marketing implementation in practice

Over the past decade practice management teams have needed to develop a range of marketing skills to ensure the practice attracts a steady stream of patients. As patients' disposable incomes have shrunk, many private or mixed practices have needed to step up their marking activities. In small businesses the marketing function draws staff away from their operational work, as, unlike in larger businesses with marketing departments the work of marketing falls upon clinicians and administrators, therefore it is important to ensure that marketing activities make optimum use of time and resources invested into them.

Computer technology underpins most dental practice's day to day operations, although often not their marketing activities, even although according to National Statistics 73% of UK homes use the internet. This is a significant fact when choosing the techniques to be used for effective marketing campaigns, in particular because internet use is linked to various socio-economic and demographic indicators, such as age, location, marital status and education, therefore it would be easy to tailor-make campaigns for particular customer groups. For example, although in 2010 60% of people aged 65 and over had never accessed the internet, 99% of people aged 16 to 24 regularly do. While 97% of adults educated to degree level had accessed the internet, only 45% without any formal qualifications had done so.

The number of adults who bought or ordered goods or services online within the previous 12 months reached 31 million in 2010. These internet shoppers represented 62% of all adults. In light of these statistics, email marketing cannot be ignored as a method of contacting existing and lapsed patients. It could also be used to contact other practices for potential referrals or local businesses to attract people to your practice who work locally.

Dental Practice Management

There are a range of tools for email marketing, some offering up to 500 emails free of charge, whilst other provide free 60 day trials, to make your e-marketing campaign simple to manage and beautifully presented. These are known as Cloud tools, two of the market leaders are Campaign Monitor and Mail Chimp. With the tools in place, to achieve the best results structure your campaigns with:

- **A progressive message** - don't just send and re-send the same message; make the emails a series, telling a tale. Plan the entire campaign in line with your campaign targets before sending the first message.
- **Clear target groups** - appropriate messages for particular client groups will differ. When the tools are available and sending is low cost, it is best to run a range of tailored campaigns.
- **Key messages** - stimulate interest by opening with a fact that will grab their attention, then give them some more information but require them to click through onto your website for the full story.
- **A call for action** - without a call for action you will not maximise results, ask them to call or email for an appointment or consultation with a treatment coordinator.

Marketing experts have discovered that the response to the first exposure to marketing information is unlikely to prompt sales, it is with spaced repetition that uptake increases, with television advertising peaking at the sixth exposure. Therefore, when you plan your campaign you need to prepare a coordinated set of four emails to be sent out on a weekly basis. However, it is important to note an unsubscribe link in your emails is essential to avoid being fined under the terms of the advertising code. The Cloud technology mentioned earlier includes this function; always act on recipient's requests to be removed from your database.

Securing your data list can be as straightforward as asking patients for their email addresses and their permission to send the information about offers and promotions. This will be especially useful to re-engage them in the event that their attendance lapses. Some practices are building relationships with local businesses who will work with them if they offer their staff sweeteners. Named contacts for personnel departments can be found on job sites and local newspapers.

When planning your campaign there are few simple rules which will increase uptake of the services promoted:

- Use a professional template, and keep the images to a minimum
- Don't make the email about you; grab their attention with what will interest them and not what you want from them
- Encourage them to visit your website
- Comply with legal and GDC advertising requirements
- Follow through with a progressive campaign.

Once you have sent out your information, analyse the results and see how many emails were opened and what action the recipients took in response. Contact Manager and Mail Chimp have tools to provide that information. You will find that sending out at certain times of the day and certain days of the week secure better response levels than others. When cold calling, as a general rule you can expect 20% of recipients to open the email and 15% to follow through with visits to your website. This number will be much higher when send out to patients who know and trust you.

Critical analysis

Audit

When the time measured span of the SMART objectives has elapsed the manager must compare the results secured with the benchmarks set in the SMART objectives. Once the project's results have been collated they can be critically analysed. This analysis is purposeful and reflective leading to judgment of the value of the results of a project. Consideration is given to the outcomes realised by the methods or techniques employed to determine future marketing activities. Critical analysis is one of the defining characteristics of professional management and should be recorded as a brief and highly readable explanation of the cause and effect of the results secured.

The audit will measure the:

- Number of e-shots sent
- Number of responses
- Number of appointments booked
- Number of treatments purchased
- Uptake of interest free finance.

Evaluation

This will measure staff and patient attitudes to the new working procedures and how they think they could be improved, using an on-going staff development and improvement basis.

Marketing is like planting seeds - some shoot up quickly then run to seed and need replanting. Others are perennials and will self-pollinate, providing glorious blooms year after year. If your marketing crops are failing then a little rotation could restore your fortunes.

Chapter 3:
Managing Quality Systems

This chapter explores theories of quality management and their application in the dental sector. Modern quality theories originated during the 1930s, since when quality theorists have introduced new and adapted existing techniques to optimise their effectiveness and efficiency. The Health and Social Care Act 2008 has reemphasised the need to make quality of care a primary concern for dental care providers. This chapter will examine of a wide range of approaches to quality management and discuss the application of techniques for assessing and developing the efficient and effective services for Care Quality Commission compliance.

Health and Social Care Act 2008

In an ideal world all dental practices would achieve the 'Gold Standard' by using the best materials and techniques for treating patients and having a fully equipped decontamination room with a wide range of safeguarding policies and protocols in place. It is beyond doubt that many practices observe 'Best Practice' in all they do, however some do not; and really should not be seeing patients at all!

For some considerable time now the idea of whole team professionalism has been considered to be the gold standard for excellent patient care and the way to enhance the job satisfaction of dental care professionals. Over recent years new initiatives such as clinical governance and dental care professional (DCP) registration have advanced this aspiration. In some practices their team ethos, along with the implementation of a wide range of team development initiatives have allowed DCPs to thrive and develop their role. Without exception these practices have benefited from their input to their teams' development. However, such practices are small in number and in the greater majority very little has changed despite dental nurse registrations and the requirements it places on registrants.

The Care Quality Commission (CQC) initiative is designed to develop quality management in dental services and provide a robust framework for whole team professionalism. From April 2010, the CQC requires all health and social care providers to register and provide evidence that they are consistently meeting the Key Performance Indicators of the 28 standards, set out in the CQC's *Essential Standards of Quality and Safety* in which the outcomes patients should experience when using a service are specified.

The CQC standards are based upon principles of quality management first developed in America during the 1930s by Edwards-Deming, an American statistician, and further developed by a wide range of theorists such as Duran and Crosby to become the theories of Total Quality Management we work with today. Although quality principles began in the USA they were further developed during the industrialisation of Japan following WWII. The Japanese adaptations to the early quality theories are known as Kaizen.

Total Quality Management (TQM)

This is a comprehensive and structured approach to organisational management that seeks to improve the quality of products and services through ongoing refinements in response to continuous feedback. TQM processes are divided into four sequential categories: plan, do, check, and act (*the PDCA cycle*). In the *planning* phase, people define the problem to be addressed, collect relevant data, and ascertain the problem's root cause; in the *doing* phase, people develop and implement a solution, and decide upon a measurement to gauge its effectiveness; in the *checking* phase, people confirm the results through before-and-after data comparison; in the *acting* phase, people document their results, inform others about process changes, and make recommendations for the problem to be addressed in the next PDCA cycle.

Kaizen is the Japanese for 'improvement' or 'change for the better' and refers to philosophy or practices that focus upon continuous improvement of processes supporting business processes, and management. It has been applied in healthcare, psychotherapy, life-coaching, government, banking and many other industries. When used in the business sense and applied to the workplace, kaizen refers to activities that continually improve all functions, and involves all employees. Kaizen influenced American business and quality management teachers who visited the country and has since spread throughout the world.

There can be no doubt that in order to observe these detailed standards practices, the involvement and cooperation of each member is needed. In particular this will make adding the role of treatment coordinator a sensible way to enable practices to allocate responsibility for the development of patient focused, quality initiatives to ensure that the practice is proactive in observing CQC outcomes numbers 1 to 3 in respect of patient involvement and informed consent.

Over recent years large numbers of dental practices have chosen to participate in quality assurance initiatives such as the BDA Good Practice and Investors in People and so are familiar with principles of continuous improvement through effective and efficient policies and procedures. For those practices the quality principles are already built into their activities and taking existing measures forward to meet the CQC standards is straightforward. When the whole team is involved in the development and audit of the standards, not only is the load shared, but individuals are committed to the success of the measures introduced.

The 28 Standards are organised into the following six sections. It is sensible for providers to allocate responsibilities to appropriate team members for example:

- **Outcome 1** - Involving and information - could be lead by **receptionists** or **treatment coordinators**
- **Outcome 2** - Personalised care, treatment and support - could be lead by **dentists** and **treatment coordinators**
- **Outcome 3** - Safeguarding and Safety - could be lead by **practice managers**
- **Outcome 4** - Suitability of staffing - could be lead by **providers** and **practice managers**
- **Outcome 5** - Quality and management - could be lead by **providers** and **practice managers**
- **Outcome 6** - Suitability of management- here in the first place, practice could take advice from a trusted advisor.

Quality gurus and their theories

There have been four generations of Quality Gurus since the 1930s:

- Founding Fathers – Americans such as Edwards-Deming in the 1930s
- Americans who took the message of quality to Japan in the late 1940s
- The Japanese Industrialists who began to develop the Kaizen concept in the 1950s
- The Western gurus who followed the Japanese industrial success from the 1970s onward.

TQM was a key feature of management during the 1980s. At that time, managers were beginning to recognise the value of basing their companies culture on 'person-centred' systems and principles.

- **TQM** = is a process for continuous management of quality
- **TOTAL** = involving everyone in all company activities
- **QUALITY** = conforming to requirements
- **MANAGEMENT** = supervision of processes and procedures.

Dr W Edwards-Deming was a statistician, professor, and consultant whose statistical background had a huge influence upon this thinking and shaped his quality management techniques. He placed great importance upon the responsibility of management both at individual and company levels. He theorised that 94% of quality problems are the responsibility of management. To address this he developed a fourteen point management philosophy, relevant to organisations of all sizes across all business sectors. These 14 points are now regarded as a 'recipe for quality', providing guidance and support for managers. They open the mind to systematic ways of thinking about the purpose of the business, its procedures and processes, whist considering the roles and needs of its people.

Deming's 14 points are not to be considered as tablets of stone. His philosophy advocates continuous review and development as guiding principles and as such Deming has continually reviewed and refined his 14-points. On a strategic level, Deming's management systems are closely linked to the statistical control of procedures and establishing clear end results for systems. On a tactical level he advocates that systems are operated on a basis of 'management by positive co-operation basis', as opposed to management by conflict. In short, this means working in a win-win, rather than a win-lose environment. The success of TQM is, according to Edwards-Deming, dependent upon the resolution of conflict and cultivation of teamwork in the workplace. Deming advocates:

> *"Best efforts are not enough; best efforts will not ensure quality"* Everyone putting forth best efforts from their own individual point of view results in much wasted labour; everyone needs to pull in the same direction, the direction which is of the greatest benefit to the company as a whole."

Another key feature of the Edwards-Deming philosophy is a concentration on the customer. Many theorists talk about 'satisfying the customer at the lowest possible cost'. Deming however writes:

> *"It will not suffice to have patients that are merely satisfied. An unhappy customer will switch. Unfortunately a satisfied customer may also switch, on the theory that he could not lose much, and may gain. Profit in business comes from repeat business, business that boasts about your product and service, and that bring their friends with them"*

To enable managers to benefit from his philosophy, Edwards-Deming provides his 14 points as 'tools to think with'.

Deming's 14 Points

1. Focus on long term needs rather than short term profitability
2. We cannot accept delays, mistakes or defects
3. Quality requires reliable, dependable, consistent procedures
4. Develop long-term team relationships that ensure the development of relevant skills, loyalty and trust
5. Improve constantly and forever, every process for planning and delivering services
6. Training must be practical and relevant. Every team member must know:
   → What their job is
   → How to do it properly
7. Leadership must be aimed toward helping people to do a better job
8. Encourage free and honest communication within the team
9. Break down barriers between departments and staff groups
10. Don't promote empty slogans or buzz words. E.g. 'zero defects'
11. Don't set quantitative targets
12. Recognise and reward pride in workmanship
13. Promote CPD
14. Demonstrate top management's commitment quality, the company and its people.

Edwards-Deming states that it is not enough to simply adopt these points, individually or collectively. Success is dependant upon using the 14 points to create an environment fully consistent with and conducive to them.

"THIS IS NOT A PROJECT OR A PROGRAMME. THIS IS NEVER ENDING AND FOREVER."

Edward Deming advocated a systematic approach to problem solving and promoted the widely known *Plan, Do, Check, Act* (PDCA) cycle. The PDCA cycle is also known as the Deming cycle, which was developed by a colleague of Deming, Dr Shewhart:

- **Plan** what is needed
- **Do** it
- **Check** that it works
- **Act** to correct any problems or improve performance.

The cycle is about learning an ongoing improvement, learning what works and what does not in a systematic way; and the cycle repeats; after one cycle is complete,

Dental Practice Management

another is started. Deming's theories open the 'quality debate'. Numerous management gurus have added their interpretations of quality, in line with the requirements of their particular business sectors. Here is a selection of interpretations from quality theorists:

Edwards-Deming	Quality is a **predictable** degree of **uniformity** and **dependability**, at **low cost** and **suited to the market**
Joseph Juran	Quality is fitness for use: Juran developed the quality trilogy - quality planning, quality control and quality improvement. Based upon the concept that good quality management requires quality actions to be planned out, improved and controlled
Philip B Crosby	Quality is conformance to requirements. Crosby is known for the concepts of 'Quality is Free' and Zero Defects' and his quality improvement process is based on his four absolutes of quality
Dr Genichi Taguchi	Quality is the (minimum) loss imparted by the product to society Believed it is preferable to design a product that is robust or insensitive to variation in the manufacturing process, rather than attempt to control all the many variations during actual manufacture
Armand V Feigenbaum	Quality is in essence a way of managing the organisation. Was the originator of 'total quality control', often referred to as total quality
Tom Peters	Identified leadership as being central to the quality improvement process, discarding the word 'Management' for 'Leadership'. The new role is of a facilitator, and the basis is 'managing by walking about' (MBWA)
British Standard Definition	Quality is the totality of features and characteristics of a product, service or process, which bear on its ability to satisfy a given need; from the patient's view point.

Each of these additions builds on Deming's original philosophy which was summarised by Robert Flood in his book *Beyond TQM* as can be summarised as:

"*Quality means* **meeting customers agreed requirements, formal and informal at the lowest cost, first time every time**"

Quality audit

Quality audit is a process for measuring the extent to which systems and procedures are:

- Achieving their objectives
- Using resources.

As this technique was introduced by Edwards-Deming, it will come as no surprise that his quality audit processes are based on statistical audit. According to Deming, quality systems must be **effective**, **efficient** and **continuously improving**.

EFFECTIVENESS: is a measured on a scale of 1 to 10 upon the extent to which the system secures the desired results. This measure is calculated with reference to the relevant policy statement, in which the objectives for the area of activity being audited are specified.

EFFICIENCY: is again a measure on the scale of 1-10 of the way the system uses resources.

The efficiency of a system is measured in the terms of:

- Economy
  How economically does the system use materials and manpower.

- Adaptability
  How the system responds when adapted response is required

- User friendliness
  How well the team are able to operate
  How easy the system is to use
  How patients experience the system

- Reliability
  How consistent are the results achieved

Managers should Quality Audit all systems regularly to ensure they are fit for purpose

Dental Practice Management

and consistently achieving the best results for patients. The span of this activity is extensive and managers should prepare a quality audit timetable to spread this work throughout the year.

Theory in practice

Implementation of quality audit processes based on the PDCA quality cycles starts with the production of benchmarks in the form of a quality statement for the system. Based on this an assessment of effectiveness and efficiency is made from which quality improvements can be determined to raise the overall score calculated when adding together the five individual scores linked to effectiveness and efficiency. It is advisable to involve all users of the system in audit and the process of planning and implementing the improvements, which will then be re-quality audited.

Quality cycle

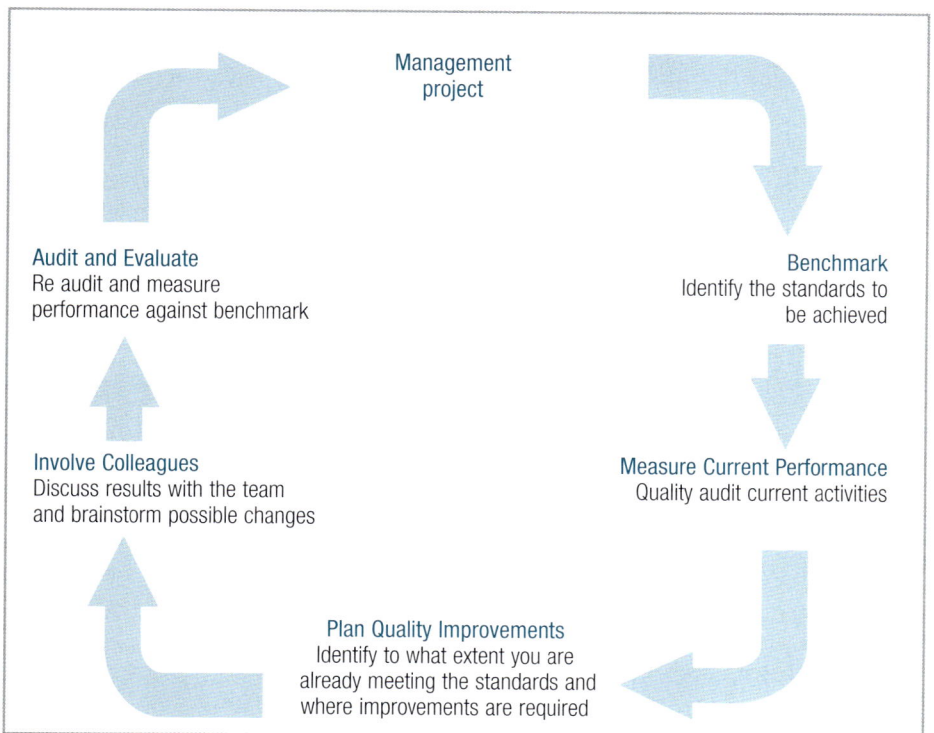

Management project

Audit and Evaluate
Re audit and measure performance against benchmark

Benchmark
Identify the standards to be achieved

Involve Colleagues
Discuss results with the team and brainstorm possible changes

Measure Current Performance
Quality audit current activities

Plan Quality Improvements
Identify to what extent you are already meeting the standards and where improvements are required

Example Quality Audit for Cross Infection Control

Effectiveness	Score out of 10	Analysis
	3	There is often a lack of clarity about who is responsible for decontamination activities. At times there too many nurses in the decontamination room, at other times nobody is available and we run out of stock and available instruments. There have been numerous incidents of instruments going missing.

Effectiveness	Score out of 10	Analysis
Economy	3	Patients have been reappointed due to lack of usable instruments and at times we have needed to obtain materials quickly, rather than economically. This is due in part to the fact that there are only 2 autoclaves and 1 washer-disinfector for 8 surgeries. One of the sterilisers is unreliable and we can't always spare the time to use the washer disinfector. There are only 2 ultrasonic baths and they are regularly overloaded with instruments.
Reliability	3	The lack of resources: equipment, staff and time mean that our decontamination processes are often deficient.
Adaptability	3	The general lack of resources and organisation mean that we are frequently unable to respond to unexpected events and the service to patients suffers as a direct result.
User friendly	1	In no way can this be considered to be user friendly unless things are changed the quality control of the processing of instruments is dubious.

Quality summary

The system has scored 13 out of a possible 50, which reflects a 26% quality rating. Were the CQC to visit they would be far from happy. On the surface the decontamination room looks well equipped with sterilisers, ultrasonic baths, and steriliser pouches etc, but if someone was to observe how the resources are being used they pick up on the points shown in the analysis above. Based on these observations a team meeting is required to discuss and action plan to rectify these shortfalls and raise the quality rating to at least 80% in the first instant, and then based on continuous improvement on to 95-100%.

Policy Process and Procedure

The strategic level of quality management is the development of a quality policy defining benchmarks through preset objectives, procedures and processes. A quality policy is an 'umbrella policy' covering a range of sub-polices each related to specific areas of activity. Together they define the operational aspect of quality management.

This begins with the strategic policy statement in the form of a general statement of intent, outlining the practice philosophy, ethic and goals. For example:

- Continuous improvement
- Company and employee attitudes
- Achieve customer satisfaction
- Identify needs
- Involve everyone
- Set service standards
- Measure results
- Continuous Professional Development
- Recognise and reward.

With a clear view of what you are working to achieve in respect of quality management you are now ready to identify the procedures that will secure success.

Tactics

Consider how you will:

- Motivate staff
- Produce clear work instructions
- Conduct quality audit procedures
- Monitor procedures
- Market research effects
- Recognise staff achievements.

Policy building

Policies are measures designed to achieve consistent management success, which is the direct result of clear management direction. In today's business environment managers need to develop an extensive range of skills to secure an appropriate balance between profitability and compliance with an extensive range of legal and ethical obligations.

Policy writing begins with a statement of purpose and goes on to identify broad guidelines for achieving the stated purpose. This is then a framework for decision making and defining implementation measures.

Policies should meet identified needs whilst reflecting the practice's beliefs, values or philosophy on the issue concerned. The policy will formulate and define simple procedures to be followed to enable a consistent and equitable approach to be adopted. Quality is compromised when no policies are in place, or when policies are vague, badly communicated, or where there is a diversity of interests and preferences resulting in conflicting objectives among those who are directly involved. Intelligent application of policy is vital, you need discretion in its implementation; however the margins for that discretion should be stated as part of the policy to prevent it from becoming impotent.

When creating a policy you should begin with the practice business plan, which is the manager's constant reference point for decision-making. A comprehensive business plan will identify where the business wants to be in one-year's time and specify how you plan to get there. It will identify targets, budgets and resources then go on to set timetables. With this valuable document in place, the manager has 'tools to think with'.

Having set your goals through business planning, a consistent pathway is required to achieve success. At this point, the manager requires agreed policies to move the plan forward. Policy making is strategic management. Policies are built on the following series of decisions about the area covered by the policy:

- **Purpose** of the policy
- **Scope** of the policy
- **Activities** required for the observation of the policy
- **Review monitoring** processes.

Dental Practice Management

This Covers

Purpose	What you hope to achieve: the outcomes the policy will achieve
Scope	State who is involved in this activity
Activities	List the actions required to achieve the aims of the policy How you will achieve the outcomes
Review	Identify the review process

Making improvements

Making improvements to deficient systems can be complex. Especially if an improvement in one area leads to deterioration in another, or when applying a solution to a problem makes the problem worse.

For example, if a system is underperforming, responding with a knee jerk solution to send the staff on a training course when the real cause of the problem is due to the procedures they are working to or something else, then a training course won't fix it.

Before making a change, use the quality cycle to understand the bigger picture; where problems occur and their domino effects. Discuss your ideas with the team; there are always people who think a change will fail. Find them and ask them why they think this, so you don't find them saying after the event, 'I could have told you why that would fail'.

David McClelland's team at Harvard summarised the requirements for any significant change to be lasting and effective as follows:

People must ...
... be willing to change (if they're not it's a motivation issue)
... be able to change (if they're not it's a training/competency issue)
... not be prevented from changing (if they are, it's a 'systemic' issue).

In my experience, I have often seen the third of these as the real blocker. Systems and procedures, both implicit and explicit, both written and unwritten, can get in the way.

When you address systemic shortfalls, staff motivation often changes in response and people will then actively seek the knowledge they need to become competent in the new way. A key measure of management success is the quality of care delivered by the practice in both clinical and non-clinical aspects of care. Managers need to be aware not only of the operational needs of the practice but must also have a clear vision of the bigger picture and base their management decisions upon it, thus ensuring consistency and fairness.

The QUIET quality-focused management process enhances consistent and focused management:

Q quality focused: requiring managers to have a benchmark for the services they provide and using it as the basis for developing the policies and procedures
U underpinning the work of the team: providing leadership and resources to ensure that as far as possible, clinicians can be patient focused and not distracted by avoidable administrative errors and cumbersome procedures
I information based management: management decisions need to be evidence based requiring managers to draw information from colleagues and patients when making management decisions
E end user focused: In addition to being evidence based, discretionary decisions should be holistically based giving consideration to the physical, social and emotional impacts upon purchasers and providers
T team driven: managers need to motivate and empower the team through good communications and positive strokes.

The role of the practice manager is both pastoral and remedial. This can mean that you are wearing many different hats, at times acting as a matrix band holding different facets of the practice together, or acting as a mentor providing support and guidance to colleagues. At other times you will need to 'grasp the nettle' to manage difficult and often emotionally charged situations. The role of manager is both demanding and rewarding for managers with the appropriate skills and support. It is all too easy for managers to focus on the needs of the patients and colleagues, whilst failing to recognise their own needs. The fact is, just like the man chopping down trees with a blunt axe, managers that stop to take time for their personal and professional development can reap the benefits and achieve better results for less effort.

Chapter 4:
Systems for Financial Management

This financial management chapter will focus on definitions for, and implementation of, financial management techniques and will show techniques for monitoring the progress toward securing financial objectives. As with all areas of management financial planning, activities should be designed to contribute to the achievement of the business' objectives as set out in the business plan. Throughout this chapter aspects of financial terminology and the use of management accounts will be shown along with the legal and regulatory measures required to structure proactive financial policies.

Glenys Bridges

The financially literate dental practice manager

In bygone days a 'sensible' approach to income and expenditure was enough to maintain a profitable dental business. At that time acceptable financial record keeping would be an accurate account of patients' payments and suppliers' bills. Some people may yearn for those bygone days, however nowadays every dental business needs a competent financial manager to optimise the practice's finances.

Alongside providing excellent patient care, dental businesses must also provide an income for the dental professionals it employs. This requires managers to set a broad span of performance objectives and monitor performance to them. Financial results, based on projected income and expenditure are an essential part of the business plan's cash flow projections set before the start of the financial year. Then, using financial governance systems, the practice manager can produce management accounts to record financial transactions and respond to variances from target, before they reach crisis proportions. Although almost every dentist is aware of their gross monthly income, many are less clear about their net profit, which is calculated by deducting operational expenses from gross income. In most cases this is due to a lack of systematic management accounting.

Financial governance is most effective when every team member has a part to play, from the most junior nurse to the clinical directors and when each team member understands their contribution to practice profitability. The practice manager's role in financial management is pivotal, it must include educating and informing the team about the 'Financial Plan' and implementing financial controls through standardised policies and procedures.

The Care Quality Commission (CQC) has set a range of Key Performance Indicators (KPIs) to measure and improve dental practice operations, one such category relates to financial performance. These indicators aim to quantify and measure the efficiency of practice operations. Financial KPIs for dental practice would include income and expenditure to target in respect of:

- Proportion of accounts receivable banked
- Operating expenses
- Average production costs per patient
- Gross production costs.

Dental Practice Management

The data collected are used to monitor performance, so that corrective action can be taken to address deviations between 'actual' values and 'target' values.

Soaring overheads can have a devastating effect on profitability. Unless effective accounting systems are in place it can be difficult to know when overhead costs such as salaries, supplies, rent, insurance, and other expenses, are too high. Excessive overheads jeopardise the success and financial security of the business. Calculating overheads as a percentage of practice revenue is important for gauging its economic health. As a practice grows, its overhead percentage should remain stable or decline, even although actual overheads may increase. Keeping the overhead percentage within range of the national average can be difficult. However, the following can help control overhead, and increase profitability in the practice:

- Follow the money

Track where the money comes from and where it goes by monitoring fees collected, purchases and expenses including salaries. This is reasonably easy to do when using one of the accounting software packages readily available. It is a good idea to ask your accountant which package they advise you to use, since when you use the system they prefer it is quicker, and therefore less expensive for them to produce your end of year tax accounts.

- Manage stock levels

During stocktaking some practices find they have disproportionate stock levels, they have laid out cash on supplies that will carry them for months, rather than using a 'just in time' stock system which can prevent expired items having been purchased that can only then be disposed of. Determine the materials used over the previous year then calculate productivity. In this way you can project requirements in the current year. Benchmarking against past performance can help a practice ensure accurate ordering of supplies to avoid waste.

- Reward performance

There are two kinds of overheads: fixed and variable. Fixed overheads must be paid no matter how the practice is performing. Variable overheads, increase only when productivity increases. Therefore a bonus system of key performance indicators is a variable overhead which when well managed offers a 'win-win' situation for the practice and its team.

Meeting the costs of doing business is part of running a practice, but only by eliminating unnecessary expenses can you ensure the financial health of the practice. Many dentists and their teams overlook opportunities to reduce costs and improve financial performance.

Financial performance is gauged by calculating the proportion of income which is profit. In 2009 the average net profit generated per Principal practitioner in a typical private dental practice was £113,576. In comparison, the average net profits generated per Principal practitioner in a typical NHS dental practice is £120,521. These figures and others provided by dental chartered accountants can be used by the practice manager to benchmark performance against the national averages.

Each year practice managers with financial responsibilities should sit down with the Principal dentist and set budgets and profit targets for each area of activity. These should be built into the cash flow forecast and translated into monthly management accounts. Management accounts determine how the practice is performing and whether any corrective action is needed.

Financial terminology

In most areas of management the practice manager role has 'come of age', even so it is surprising how many managers still have restricted access to information about the practice's finances. Large numbers of practice managers are not allowed full access to financial data. This restricts their ability to manage as they are not able to base management decisions upon hard financial facts. With a restricted view of the bigger picture, they cannot make evidence-based decisions to secure the practices' profitability. A lesson to be learned from the international financial melt down is that we cannot afford to be nonchalant when it comes to business finances. Now is the time for practice managers without formal training in business finance to up their game and become financially literate. At the very least they need to maintain an overview of the practice's financial health by using monthly management accounts and acting upon the Notes to the Accounts (the financial review your practice accountants produce as the rationale for your accounts.)

Financial literacy

The accounting world has a language of its own, which can seem impenetrable to those of us who have not spent years studying its intricacies. Nevertheless, solid financial rationale should underpin all business decisions, so it is essential to become financially literate. Essentially this begins with learning how to read the practice accounts and pick-up and respond to trends. This requires a working knowledge of the following financial reports:

1 Profit and Loss Accounts (P&L)

Also known as the income statement, P&L accounts show income received from the sale of goods and services, along with the cost of sales - how much you have spent to generate this income. This includes staff wages, materials and overheads. The role of the manager is to ensure the percentage increase in costs is less than the percentage increase in revenue, in which case you have controlled your direct cost base. The aim is to calculate the operating profit, the money earned from your business activities after deducting direct cost of sales and indirect expenses; showing profitability.

2 Balance sheets

This gives the practice's financial position at a specified point in time: it shows the total value of business assets (what the business owns), less liabilities (what the business owes). There are several ways to calculate these figures. Traditionally the price paid for assets has been used in this calculation, although in the current financial climate, it can be more provident to use the market value of assets at a given time to prevent assets from being over valued and so making the balance sheet meaningless. When all liabilities have been settled, the remaining value of the practice's assets is known as equity.

3 Cash flow statement

This is the most important working document, which should be consulted by practice managers on a day- to- day basis for decision making. It tracks the actual movement of cash into and out of a business over a financial period. This is in contrast to the profit and loss, which records income when it is earned and expenses when they are due for payment, whether or not the cash has been received/paid. It is not unknown for businesses with a healthy P&L to go under; because the money they need to settle with their creditors is not immediately available, although it has been earned but not paid to the business.

4 Notes to accounts

Practice managers need to be able to interpret the information provided in the financial documents discussed above. They also need to be able to read between the lines of the annual accounts produced by the practice accountants. Annual accounts will be supplemented by Notes to the Accounts. These notes provide background information, such as how decisions on the value of assets have been reached. Many company owners read financial statements from back to front, in this way they can understand the underpinning judgements before looking at actual results.

Each of these financial statements needs to be considered in conjunction with each other to give an insight of the financial health of the practice.

> "Business success might not be determined by how many customers you have, the quality of your product, the price or many other things – it might be down to a simple case of managing your cash flows!' .

Dental businesses need to closely monitor their cash flow. Cash is the life blood of all businesses and is the primary indicator of business health. Most businesses can survive several periods of making a loss, but they can only run out of cash once. Cash flow is crucial at times when access to cash is difficult and expensive as in the present economic climate. In its simplest form, cash flow is the movement of money in and out of your business. It is not profit and loss, although trading clearly has an effect on cash flow. The effect of cash flow is real, immediate and, if mismanaged, totally unforgiving. More businesses fail for lack of cash than for want of profit and is the single most important reason why many businesses fail, regardless of how good the business is. Therefore, cash needs to be monitored, protected, controlled and put to work.

Accounting

Management accounts – usually comprise of an overview of the businesses progress over a stated period of time, in comparison with previous comparable periods. There is no rule as to what financial information is presented or how, as these accounts are for internal use only, to assist the company directors with managing the business. Usually prepared monthly **management accounting** or **managerial accounting** is concerned with providing managers with information to base business decisions upon, that will allow them to meet the business objectives set out in the business plan.

Dental Practice Management

Management accounting information is:
- Designed and intended exclusively for use by managers within the organiaation
- Usually confidential not publicly reported
- Forward-looking, instead of historical
- Determined on a needs basis, rather than in line with general financial accounting standards.

Record Keeping

Numerous computerised bookkeeping software packages are widely used in modern businesses. In most cases businesses will chose their software package after taking their accountant's advice.

Expenditure – management accounts Accounting Year – 1 April 3000 to 31 March 3001

Budget Area	Annual Budget	Month - May 3000	Year to date	Variance
Wages	£200,000.00	£15,000.00	£30,000.00	+ £3,333.00
Materials	£500,000.00	£45,000.00	£105.000.00	(£21,666.00)
Communications	£25,000.00	£2,000.00	£5,000.00	(£ 833.00)
Marketing	£10,000.00	£5,000.00	£6,000.00	(£4,333.00)
Insurances	£5,000.00	£600.00	£3,600.00	(£2,766.00)
Professional services	£10.000.00	£1,500.00	£1,500.00	+£166.00
Totals	£750.000.00	£69,100.00	£156,100.00	(£29,600)

N.B. For the purpose of giving an example the figures in this table have been rounded up. Actual accounts would be accurate to the penny.

Bracketed numbers show over spends to date '+' - figures show budgets not fully spent.

Income management accounts Year -1 April 3000 to 31 March 3001

Budget Area	Annual Budget	Month - May 3000	Year to date	Variance
NHS	£215,000.00	£18,000.00	£36,000.00	(£166.67)
Private Patients	£600,000.00	£45,000.00	£95.000.00	£5,000.00
Surgery Rental to consultants	£24,000.00	£ 2,000.00	£4,000.00	£0
Sundry goods sales	£12,000.00	£ 900.00	£1,500.00	£500.00
Totals	£851,000.00	£65.900.00	£136,500.00	£5,333.33

Bracketed numbers show income shortfalls to date '+' - figures show better than forces performance

Cash Flow

Cash flow management – Cash flow management is all about balancing the cash coming into the business with the cash going out. Unmanaged there is a danger that cash inflows lag behind the cash outflows, leaving the business short of cash. This money shortage is the cash flow gap. When a business is trading profitably, each time the cycle turns, a little more money is put back than flows out of the business. Difficulties occur if corrective action is not taken when needed. When cash flow is monitored managers are able to forecast business outgoings and ensure the cash is available to meet them.

The cash flow cycle – Any dental practice uses cash to acquire resources. Those resources are put to work and goods and services produced. These are then sold to customers. You collect their payments and make those funds available for investment in new resources, and so the cycle repeats.

- **Inflows** – Cash inflow is money coming into the business:
- **Outflows** – Cash outflow is, naturally, what you pay out

Break Even

Business managers must always be aware of their break-even requirements which are calculated from of the income statement and cash flow statements to define the sales needed to meet all of your fixed and variable expenses. Break-even analysis can help you when projecting when you'll make a profit, deciding how much to charge for procedures and setting sales targets.

Capital Expenditure

This is the term applied to money spent on acquiring permanent assets - such as buildings, or equipment - that are necessary for the running of the business, anything that lasts for more than a year can be called capital expenditure.

Revenue Expenditure

Money spent to run the business. This includes cost of stock, and expenses like heating bills and can be split into 2 categories:

Fixed expenses are expenses that you'd have regardless of the level of sales of products or services (e.g. sales, rent, insurance, maintenance contracts, etc.).

Variable expenses are incurred in direction to the amount of products or services provided (e.g. consumables, utilities, tax, etc.).

Budget Management – When financial controls are delegated it is essential practice managers are given defined budgets to work within. A budget depicts what you expect to spend (expenses) and earn (revenue) over a time period. Amounts are organised into categories, activities, or accounts (for example, telephone costs, salaries, materials etc.). Budgets are essential for forecasting and monitoring whether practice finances are running to plan. They are also useful for projecting how much money you'll need for future initiatives. The overall format of a budget is a record of planned income and planned expenses for a fixed period of time. In the format of a cash flow forecast.

Cash flow forecast – The cash flow forecast, or budget projects your business cash inflows and outflows over a certain period of time. It can help you see potential cash flow gaps and allows you to take steps to avoid expensive uncontrolled overdrafts, or being unable to meet crucial payments such as wages. For dental businesses a six-month cash flow budget is required. At a bare minimum, all businesses should be able to make an accurate cash forecast for 13 weeks ahead, long enough to spot potential problems and capture quarterly costs, but short enough to be realistic on sales and debt collections. This ought to be a rolling forecast, re-calculated weekly or even daily, and is particularly useful when the business is under stress or during a credit crunch.

A cash flow forecast consists of:
- Projected cash inflows (a realistic assumption of income, based on a previous period with adjustments)
- Projected cash outflows (payments you'll need to make : operating expenses such as rents, taxes, wages and utility bills falling due)
- A profit and loss projection, when the net cash flow is added to or subtracted from opening bank balances, any likely funding gaps can be quantified.

When a negative cash flow gap is predicted early enough, it is more likely that you can take steps to manage it for example:

In the short term (over the next four weeks): Remedial action
- Encourage patients to make cash payments
- Collect all fees before treatment
- Check stock levels and place a hold on non essential purchases
- Only make immediate payments to suppliers when worthwhile discounts apply
- Reduce variable costs where possible
- Seek outside sources of cash, such as a short-term loan
- Produce and analyse management accounts

In the middle term (4 weeks to 6 months ahead): Conciliatory action
- Evaluate patient payment procedures and the payment performance of patients
- Introduce inventory management- set optimum operational stock levels
- Recalculate your hourly rate
- Ensure your prices cover the costs of production,; plus profit
- Increase the credit taken from suppliers
- Make medium and short term cash flow forecasts and update them regularly
- Review staffing levels
- Promote high end treatments
- Monitor management accounts
- SWOT analyse performance

In the long term: Beyond 6 months – Business planning
- Calculate the Return on Investment (ROI) for major purchases
- Compare bank facilities on offer to reduce charges
- Sell off or return obsolete equipment or materials
- Consider ways to develop a competitive edge

Dental Practice Management

- Regularly assess the PESTLE elements affecting your business

Cash is the life blood of businesses. At any given time the manager should be able to produce accurate and current income and expenditure figures. These should then be viewed in conjunction with working budgets for the practices operation, it is advisable to also produce best possible case projections, (the most you can earn with the resources available) and worst possible case projections (the absolute minimum for business survival), plus your working projections. The quality of these projections will be completely determined by the standard and reliability of the underlying research. An impressive set of projections is of little benefit if it is unrealistic, or based on mere speculation.

Pricing dental services

In all businesses there must be a strong link between price and the customers perception of 'value'. Although price is an objective fact and value is a subjective judgement, people will pay more for goods and services which they consider to be value for money, so as part of the pricing strategy' for dental businesses must be to understand what patients value and work to educate patients so they fully appreciate the value of oral wellbeing.

Each dental procedure has related operating costs. When you know your operating costs you can determine the fees you need to charge your patients. If you are working to a capped budget, raising fees will not be an option, in which case controlling costs will be the only way to rectify shortfalls. When you are aware of the significance of hourly production, you realise how important it is to make optimum use of the time available, through effective use of the appointment book. To calculate how much hourly income it takes to run a treatment room, we need to determine how costs to run per hour. This is calculated by listing all outgoings over the year dividing this by the number of operational hours. With this information you can assess how well the fees currently being charged will cover these outgoings.

For example one treatment room fully booked would typically provide about 30 hours per week for 46 weeks per year of 'chargeable dentistry'. There are of course many other hours spent in administration, staff meetings, staff training, postgraduate courses, holidays, days off sick, etc, but these hours do not attract any payment. In addition to the operating costs the dentist's wages and a profit margin need to be incorporated.

Dental practices exist to care for patient's dental wellbeing, to do this they must be profitable. Good financial managers can organise the business in a financially prudent manner. This will often require them to make tough spending decisions, distinguishing between the essentials and the nice to haves. This will involve making spending choices which increase costs, such as opting to use a premium price lab for their best quality prosthetics, or investing in employing consultants to make certain areas of the business more profitable.

Financial Management in Practice

Financial management begins with the business plan, where budgetary targets and financial targets are set out. The manager will then use this figures, plus management accounts prepared so that comparisons between targets and results will show variance to determine how individual areas are performing. This information is then used to direct spending decisions.

An analysis of the actual monthly cash flow results budget chart will help the manager ask the right questions to get to grips with determine reasons why areas are under or over budget, so they can determine ways to improve conditions, and to show where existing measures are working or not.

Techniques

When reviewing management accounts, a SWOT analysis will determine where and how the practice has achieved its financial objectives and show where things are not so good, to enable an action plan to be drawn up to take the business forward as efficiently as possible in the following month.

On a monthly basis the manager should recap on corrective activities to quantify the results of the previous month's adjustments to enable further analysis of how successful the practice has been financially.

Further analysis should be made on a monthly basis to determine how they compare with results form the same period in the previous year; this data should be considered with reference to your PESTLE analysis.

Along side monthly reviews, the end of year review should be conducted when the annual accounts have been finalised to provide the required information to enable

Dental Practice Management

analysis of the practices financial management. The following analysis is an example of predicted budgetary targets, the actual figures and the variance between these figures. In many practices although some expenses will exceed the budget, overall the practice may have reduce its overall expenditure, Analysis of this could be as follows.

Analysis of the areas of improved performance:
- **Hygienists** – hours were increased hence more income targets were exceeded
- **Materials** – this variable cost was further managed by negotiating materials at best prices and introducing training to reduce wastage.
- **Stationary** – costs have been reduced by purchasing professional software to design and printing literature in-house on an as needed basis
- **CPD** – the CPD budget has been stretched by including team meetings and free CPD such as instance lunch and learns to meet targets easily. Nobody has wanted to do any expensive courses this year as everyone has been satisfied with the free and cheap resources
- **Maintenance** – in house training in equipment care has reduced repair costs
- **Advertising** – the monthly payments for our yell advert were renegotiated down
- **Telephone** – By visiting a price comparison website I was able to make big reduction in our costs, Over the year a saving has been made which isn't as much as I hoped, however free texts have been used to remind patients of their appointments resulting in less failures and wasted time.
- **Electricity** – I have switched companies to get a cheaper rate but also have been on a drive to be environmentally efficient.

Analysis of poor performance areas:
- **Therapist** – due to maternity leave and sickness, therapy hours were less than projected
- **Lab fees** – have increased due to a change in supplier. Due to the high volume of work we send them I shall try to re-negotiate our rates
- **Accounting** – our accountants have raised their fees
- **IT** – new software and networking costs have taken us over budget in this area. Some of the computers needed their memory expended. This was essential expenditure as we would have lost money if the computers went down.

Overview

The current economic climate has made its mark on our financial results. We have seen fewer patients due to redundancies, people putting things on hold while finances are strained. A number of patients have been lost; some opting to go to an NHS dentist for cheaper treatment, whereas others crossing their fingers and hoping not to have a dental emergency. Those patients that attend are spending less on optional treatments to save money.

The recession is hitting us hard; expenses are escalating: the prices of some materials have almost double, plus HTM and CQC preparedness have taken us over budget.

> 'Dentists expenses including the costs of the building, dental equipment, staff and materials, have 'risen dramatically' according to new figures from the NHS information centre. Practice principals saw their expenses increase by 7.6 percent from £218,000 in 2007/08 to £235,500 in 2008/09'

On this basis my action plan is to:
- Pursue all possible discounts
- Keeping waste to a minimum
- Considering buying when materials are on offer
- Sourcing cheaper insurances etc
- Providing the best quality service possible to keep our patients and hopefully gain more through recommendation

One area to explore to ensure the practice operates more effectively is that of raising our fees to increase the income and in turn increase the profit.

> 'At the cheaper price you make less profit because the product brings in less revenue, and at the more expensive end you will make less profit because you sell less.'

The above quote demonstrates clearly how price increase needs to be made with care as they could actually have a detrimental effect on business, especially with the current economic climate people are looking for reductions and therefore special offers rather than increases could raise the amount of work done.

Along with setting the budget for the practice based upon the previous years financial results I set corrective actions of:
- Profit – aim to increase profit from 20% to at least 30%
- Materials – aim to decrease expenditure from 12% of turnover to 10%
- Maintenance – aim to decrease expenditure from £6500 to £3500 for the year

- Stationary – aim to decrease expenditure from £2500 to £2400 for the year – only a small decrease but relevant and achievable for the receptionist so as not to create barriers

Current year's financial results:	Next year's target results:
● Profit = 20% of turnover	● Profit = 30% of turnover
● Materials =12% of turnover	● Materials = 10% of turnover
● Lab fees = 4% of turnover	● Lab fees = 4% of turnover
● Maintenance = £6500 which included HTM arrangements	● Maintenance = £3500
● Stationary/postage = £2500	● Stationary/postage = £1000
● CPD = £1000	● CPD = £300

'The effective management of cash and working capital will increase profits and reduce the risk of embarrassment or, even worse, business failure.'

The above statement raises an important point that finances need to be managed by monitoring to ensure money is available from profits to cover the expenditure needed to make further profits as without this control the business could fail.

As well as looking at the figures for the year it is essential to look at the key figures each month to determine any patterns and to show how well the practice is managing the accounts on a monthly basis:

We can conclude from the above chart that when monitoring performance on a monthly basis the results fluctuate with quite a variance. If one month performs well with its income it is common to see the next month perform slightly poorer on its expenses due to replacing used materials. Many months may not have had any expenses on CPD, stationary or maintenance as these are purchased when required resulting in some months being high. For these reasons it is essential to also record all the results as a year report to give final figures that show whether targets have been met over the year which is more important than individual months when there is such a fluctuation. However by recording monthly it ensures that the practice accounts are

being pro-actively monitored to enable warning signs to be read and acted upon
In conclusion the management accounting system has been effective in both monitoring/controlling the practice finances and in its results in decreasing expenditure to make the most out of what has been a hard year financially. Without this system in place the financial results could have been worse.

Chapter 5:
Ongoing Team Development

This chapter looks a range of personnel management techniques that dental employers can implement to create productive and motivated teams. The focus is on the need to manage internal and external influences so that a compliant, equitable workplace culture can be created.

Glenys Bridges

Team development needs

Each registered dental professional must demonstrate a commitment to maintaining their knowledge and skills; to this end the General Dental Council (GDC) stipulates minimum standards of training and continuing professional development (CPD) for dental professionals. The GDC defines CPD as, *"Study, training courses, seminars, reading and other activities undertaken by a dental professional, who could reasonably be expected to advance his or her development as a dental professional".*

Standards for Dental Professionals can be downloaded from their website (www.gdc-uk.org). It must be emphasised that the Standards state the minimal requirements.

The statutory role of the GDC is to protect patients and maintain confidence in dental professionals. The Dentists Act of 1921 first established a regulatory body for dentistry and required it to set standards of education and behaviour, to register dentists and regulate dentistry. Successive Dentists Acts have expanded their regulatory function and on 1 August 2008 the GDC became responsible for the registration of five additional groups of dental professionals, dental nurses were one of the new groups of dental professionals registered at this time, whose registration obliges them to meet CPD requirements.

The ultimate aim of CPD is ensure dental professionals are able to provide the best possible standards of patient care, by ensuring the registrant's professional knowledge and that they are up-to-date. Additionally, they ensure and that each dental professional's performance and behaviour meet the standards required to remain on the Dentists Register or the Dental Care Professionals (DCP) Register. Those standards specify that CPD should be completed in these two formats, verifiable and general CPD.

Verifiable CPD

This has:

- Concise educational aims and objectives
- Clear anticipated outcomes
- A quality control mechanism
- Documentary proof of evidence of completion / participation
- Covering minimum requirements in core and recommended subjects to include:
  – Medical emergencies

Dental Practice Management

– Disinfection and decontamination
– Radiography and radiation protection
– If working in a clinical environment further recommended subjects include legal and ethical issues, and handling complaints.

General CPD

This is defined as self-directed activities which provide professional development. The GDC also recommends that all dental professionals ensure that their CPD is relevant to their practice and predetermined in a Personal Development Plan.

Making the most of CPD

There can be no doubt that there is a direct link between the quality of care experienced by patients and the quality of team work in any given practice. When the practice management recognises the benefits of bringing together a group of professionally minded people with a wide range of skills and aptitudes, giveing each team member a well defined role, ongoing training and support, then it is likely that each person will excel, and the quality of patient care will be excellent.

CPD has become an integral part of maintaining the professionalism of GDC registrants and its requirements have fuelled the development of a wide range of programmes, aiming to ensure that core subject training is readily available for dental teams. Meeting the minimum standard of professional development is just the beginning, going beyond the basic requirements and defining the optimum CPD standard for your practice is what sets the good practices apart from excellent practices; below are 10 ways for you to enable your team to excel through CPD.

Include CPD in your business plan
The practice business plan is the strategic basis of all practice activities. To achieve business plan objectives requires the implementation of policies and budgets for each area of activity, including CPD. The need for structured management has been brought into sharp focus by CQC registration; in that policies and procedures must be in place.

Plan your team's CPD
Develop a team development policy based on SMART objectives for the practice and each person. The objective of CPD is to maintain patients' confidence in dental

professionals. Dental professionals are required to participate in study, training courses, seminars, reading and other activities, which could reasonably be expected to advance their development as a dental professional. In setting this requirement the GDC provides a clear mandate for managers to base practice policy upon.

Choose CPD themes for the whole team to cover each year
The benefits of CPD are undermined when individuals randomly select their learning activities rather than following a bigger plan linked to practice objectives. When CPD is entirely self-selected, people choose to lean about the things they like best, rather than those which strengthen areas in which they have a development need, thus reducing the overall benefit of their CPD. The CPD selected for any given year should be based upon appraisal outcomes and statutory requirements.

Make team meetings a CPD activity
The GDC sets out criteria for verifiable CPD. Activities should have pre-set aims and outcomes, which are evaluated by participants at the end of the activity and a register of attendees should be kept by the organiser. It is straightforward for practices to meet these and award verifiable CPD for participation in staff meetings. It would not be unreasonable to ask that participants make a contribution to the proceedings to gain their CPD certification.

Hold team debriefs after CPD activities, for reflective practice
When a team member attends CPD activities outside the practice it is beneficial for both the attendee and their team colleagues to give a reflective review of their leaning from that activity at a team meeting. Reflective practice is a central part of ongoing development as it helps to evaluate and reinforces learning.

Ensure good records are kept
Registrants are responsible for maintaining a record of their CPD. Nevertheless it is prudent for the practice to hold a record of each person's CPD. If a personal development plan is agreed as part of the annual appraisal, then it is a good idea to schedule a series of progress reviews throughout the year at which remedial action can be taken if needed.

Ensure your team log their general CPD as well as their verified CPD
Alongside the formal verifiable CPD, team members should be encouraged to log time spent in general CPD activities such as reading journals and networking. For CPD to be

eligible for inclusion, dental professionals need to set outcomes for the activities and keep a record of the subject covered and time spent. Again, keeping and sharing a reflective review is best practice for optimising learning.

Use free CPD options blended with formal educational events
Training providers are constantly looking for ways to add value to their clients learning experiences, for example The Dental Resource Company offers its learner's verifiable, core CPD for measured participation on its on-line student discussion groups. There are other opportunities for on-line free or very low cost CPD (e.g. www.shancocksltd.com) which can help stretch the CPD budget considerably.

Make it fun, with quizzes and team building activities
Having fun together is an important way to bond as a team. Teams can feel the pressure in negative ways if they are not given the chance to 'let off steam'. Ideally, teams need to have the chance to gain insight of each other's needs and expectations. There are many companies who offer innovative, exciting team building activities or, if this is beyond your CPD budget, there are excellent books to give practice managers ideas on how to integrate team building activities into regular team meetings.

Visit trade shows to see the cutting edge of the profession
The profession's major conferences and trade shows all offer CPD workshops. Although the chance to gather a year's supply of home care products from your visit is no longer available, gathering valuable CPD is, added to which it gives dental professionals insight into what is happening within their profession.

Team Development Systems

The key to successful people development lies in good communication processes and a clear understanding and application of the following management techniques.

Business Planning	• The whole process begins with the business plan in which you define the practice's philosphy and objectives
Inductions and Job Descriptions	• Once set, the vision needs to be communicated with each person's contribution to its sucessfull achievement
Policy and Procedure	• Polices and standard procedures are needed to ensure fair and equitable management
Appraisals	• Every team member should have directive and remedial feedback on their perfomance of all tasks set out in their job description
Support	• All measures agreed during an appraisal should be followed through and assessed at the next appraisal meeting to build trust and confidence
Evaluation and Review	• End with formal, written evaulations of the appraisal round completed by each person involved. The results to be taken into account when planning the next round of appraisals

Before staff developmental needs can be determined the practice's aims and objectives must be carefully set out in the business plan. Many businesses try to operate without such a clearly defined document to underpin the decision making processes. This can often be to their cost as a well defined business plan gives the practice focus, direction and provides an excellent communication channel.

Dental Practice Management

Communication channels – the communication chain

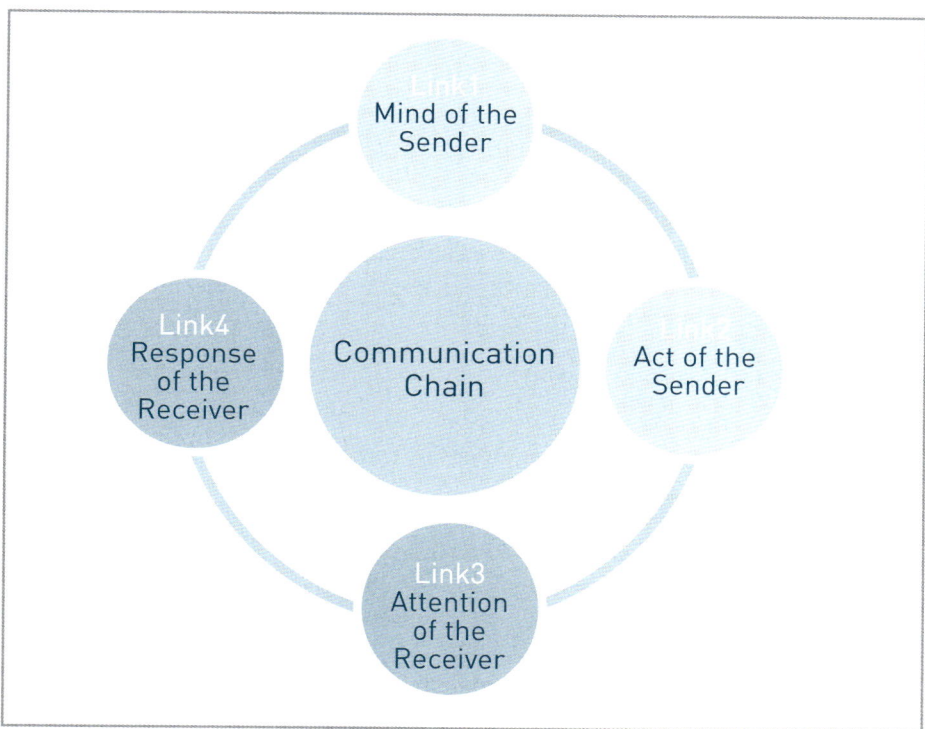

The Communication Chain theory is based on the fact that a chain is only as strong as its weakest link. It views communication as a series of linked stages, with a failure at any stage preventing the communication from moving onto the next link.
The Communication Chain, is a four-staged process, which recognises that senders and receivers must play an equal and opposite role for communication to work and must consider how their words and actions will affect the end result.

The first two links of the communication chain depend on the actions of the 'Sender'. These are the proactive stages of communication. Links three and four are the reactive stages involving the activities of the 'Receiver' as messages are received and interpreted. Having interpreted the message the receiver may well choose to send a response, which will require activities from links one and two of the communication chain.

Link One: The Mind of the Sender
At this stage it is essential for the sender to plan the communication and identify the required end results, before taking action. When you know what you want from the communication you can decide how to increase the chances of achieving the desired results. This holds as true in simple communications such as inviting a patient through to the treatment room, as it does in more complicated communications such as expressing an idea or opinion. At this stage of the communication chain the sender needs to:

- Decide upon the action or response required from the other person
- Choose the right method of communication
- Choose the right language
- Make sure that the message is clear.

Link Two: The Act of the Sender
Here the sender follows-through their thinking from link one. Actions at this link need to be based on consideration of others needs, so you need to choose a suitable time, place and way to communicate. Choosing the right timing and format for the communication is essential. At this stage of the communication chain the sender needs to ensure they are effectively responding to:

- The pre-set aims and objectives
- The sender and receiver's needs and expectations.

Link Three: The Attention of the Receiver
Communication cannot be achieved unless both parties participate actively in the communication process. Before a message can be interpreted, it must be received. This stage of the chain depends on the document being, seen and understood. People tend to have a short attention span so the format must be interesting and accessible.

Link Four: Mind of the Receiver
The receiver will have their own agenda into which they will fit the information you give them. It is essential that the messages are clear and unambiguous; it is advisable to recap and summarise important information.

Job descriptions

Once the communication techniques are in place the content of the communication must be defined. Before CQC requirements defined team roles, staff employed in dental businesses often worked without any clear idea of what their employer expected from them. In short they did not have a specified job description. This means that they had never discussed with their employer exactly what contribution was expected from them for the smooth running of the business.

When the practice seems to be running well, directing time and energy into unnecessary tasks seems pointless. Couple this with concerns that with a job description in place, certain members of staff could respond to requests to perform additional duties by saying 'It's not in my job description!' and the idea of formalising job descriptions becomes even less attractive.

Once job descriptions have been identified, they should be formalised on paper and the employer and employee should sign to say they are aware of the content. These signatures then represent both parties understanding that they are required to have and maintain the competences required to fulfil these tasks. Job descriptions should define:

- The general tasks, or functions and responsibilities of a position
- To whom the position reports
- Qualifications, skills and aptitudes required
- A person specification.

Meaningful job descriptions are developed by conducting a job analysis, to define the tasks and sequences of tasks necessary to perform the job to specify the areas of knowledge and skills needed to perform the job.

The building blocks of teamwork – Bruce Tuckman's theory of team dynamics

The quality of teamwork and team spirit are closely linked. In a group situation individuals are influenced to behave in certain ways. The role of management is to enable the team to grow, face up to challenges, tackle problems, find solutions, plan work and deliver results. Tuckman's model has become the basis for subsequent models of team dynamics and frequently used management theory to predict and manage behaviour of existing teams.

Stage 1 – Forming
- Members gather information about tasks and rules
- Leadership is evaluated
- Group members are deciding whether to integrate

Stage 2 – Storming
- Internal conflict occurs, as members form a hierarchy
- Leadership is tested
- Cliques can form to exclude certain team members

Stage 3 – Norming
- Conflict is settled, new norms develop
- Individuals conform to new norms
- Groups are formed to include team members

Stage 4 – Performing
- Teamwork is achieved, roles are flexible
- The team develops its identity and belonging grows

Stage 5 – Adjourning
- A stage of mourning at the end of a project, or when a member leaves the team
- The team will re-form when a new project or person is introduced

When the manager can see the signs of behaviour outlined for each stage of the process they are then able to act to move the team on through the process so that they settle into the productive performing stage.

Dental Practice Management

New staff inductions

The induction of all new staff is an essential process that aims to enable new team members of all levels to integrate and adapt to the culture of their new work place. The induction begins at the interview when first impressions are formed on both sides.

Induction aims to:
- Put the recruit at ease
- Create interest in the job
- Help the recruit to perform well and be happy in their job
- Induction is an important phase in the training of new staff and although time consuming, is time well spent if done properly
- What they need to know.

Experience shows that little detail of the information provided to new employees on their first day in a job is remembered. Therefore the manager should:
- Deal firstly with all personal matters affecting their health and safety
- Explain their job and how their work role fits into the overall organisation
- Ensure they are introduced to all of their colleagues and know who to go to with questions.

It is advisable to feed information to new staff on a 'little and often' basis, to build confidence and understanding. When possible support all verbal information with written documents they can retain. Since the induction process leads into the first appraisal, it is important to keep clear records of events.

Induction case study
The practice was delighted when they managed to recruit a new highly experienced, qualified nurse who had just moved into the area.

As she was qualified, she was asked to arrive just 5 minutes before staring work on her first day of employment. Within 5 minutes of her arrival she was working at the chairside.

By lunchtime on the first day the receptionist was complaining that the new nurse was constantly asking questions; although the dentist she was working with was delighted with her work.

An atmosphere began to develop, most noticeably at lunch times. Before long the new nurse began to go home for lunch. Two weeks later the new worker gave in her notice.

Ongoing Team Development

Appraisals

Although surveys reveal that few employers are 'satisfied' with their performance review or appraisals systems they are a well-established personnel management technique. Managers should invest time and energy to ensure performance reviews provide opportunities to enhance work performance and relationships.

The purpose of appraisals is to:

- Enable staff and managers to be more effective
- Recognise the achievements of staff and managers
- Conduct a performance related overview of the practice
- Identify developmental opportunities
- Identify further goals.

At their best appraisals can be very motivating and rewarding for both parties but first you must recognise that an appraisal *is not* a substitute for daily supervision *nor is it* part of a disciplinary process. An appraisal is ongoing professional development for individuals and for the team and works best when practice policy defines when, where and who is involved in the appraisal process. A suggested process is as follows:

Inform – Send the appraisee a letter of notification setting the time and place and purpose of the meeting.

Venue – Ensure the meeting is planned to take place somewhere private and free from interruptions.

Layout – Layout has a huge influence on atmosphere and mood. Create a relaxed situation, preferably at a meeting table, or in easy chairs, ideally sit at a 90 degree angle to each other to avoid face to face confrontation.

Introduction – Relax the appraisee by opening with a positive statement, smile, be warm and friendly, it is your responsibility to create a calm and non-threatening atmosphere. Explain what will happen - encourage a discussion and as much input as possible from the appraisee - tell them it is *their* meeting not yours. Open with some general discussion about how things have been going. Ask if there are any additional points to cover and note them down so as to include them when appropriate.

Review and Measure – Review the activities, tasks, objectives and achievements one by one, keeping to distinct, separate items and avoid going off on tangents or vague unspecific views. If you have done your preparation correctly you will have an order to follow. If something off-subject comes up then note it down and say you'll return to it later (and ensure you do). Concentrate on hard facts and figures and solid evidence and avoid conjecture, anecdotal or non-specific opinions, especially about the appraisee. Being objective is one of the greatest challenges for the appraiser - as with interviewing, resist judging the appraisee in your own image, according to your own style and approach - facts and figures are the acid test and provide a good neutral basis for the discussion, free of bias and personal views. For each item agree a measure of competence or achievement as relevant, and according to whatever measure or scoring system is built into the appraisal system. This might be simply a yes or no, or it might be a percentage or a mark out of ten, or an A, B, C. Reliable review and measurement requires reliable data and if you don't have the reliable data you can't review and you might as well re-arrange the appraisal meeting. If a point of dispute arises, you must get the facts straightened out before making an important decision or judgement, and if necessary defer to a later date.

Agree and action plan – An overall plan should be agreed with the appraisee, which should take account of the job responsibilities, the appraisee's career aspirations and the practice's priorities. The plan can be staged if necessary with short, medium and long term aspects, but importantly it must be agreed and realistic.

Agree specific objectives – These are the specific actions and targets that together form the action plan. As with any delegated task or agreed objective these must adhere to the SMART rules - Specific, Measurable, Agreed, Realistic, and Time-bound.

Agree necessary support – This is the support required for the appraisee to achieve the objectives, and can include training of various sorts (external courses and seminars, internal courses, coaching, mentoring, secondment, shadowing, distance-learning, reading, watching videos, attending meetings and workshops, workbooks, manuals and guides); anything relevant and helpful that will help the person develop towards the standard and agreed task.

Record main points, agreed actions and follow-up – Swiftly follow-up the meeting with all necessary copies and confirmations, and ensure a copy of the final agreement goes to the appraisee and a further copy goes into the appraisee's personnel file

Giving feedback

Performance feedback can be given as praise or criticism, both of which are judgments about performance, effort or an outcome. Always ensure that feedback is constructive and based on evidence, rather than opinions or feelings. Constructive feedback is:

- Information-specific
- Issue-focused
- Based on evidence.

It comes in two varieties:
Recognition – of good work and achievements
Remedies – this should be thought of as remedial support.

Recognition feedback should:
- Firstly identify the topic or issue that the feedback is about
- Then provide the details, without details feedback is vague and unfocused.

The way in which you say something carries more weight than what you say. Be direct when delivering your message and:

Avoid: 'Should' phrases because they only imply remedies. For example, 'Jane, you should check patients' medical histories and contact details every visit'. This is not really performance feedback. It implies that Jane did not do something well, but it doesn't provide directive feedback.

Avoid: 'Yes, but' messages. For example, 'Sarah, you have worked hard on this project, but...' What follows is the real point of the message. Words like 'but,' 'however' and 'although,' create contradictions. In fact, putting 'but' in the middle tells the other person, 'Now here is the real message'.

Appreciation expressed on its own is simple praise. When strengthened by the specifics of constructive feedback, the appraisee can recognise the message is more powerful.

Remedial feedback:
When feedback is negative it pays to take time to get your thoughts in order. This may mean delaying the feedback to give you thinking time to ensure your feedback comes

across as constructive. Always keep clear notes on the feedback given so that you can then review details of your feedback in future, rather than relying on your memory.

Interview techniques

To focus attention on the appraisee ask open-ended questions, with a focus on the issues being addressed and concentrate on one issue at a time to maintain clarity.

An appraisal should never introduce criticism that has not already been addressed through the daily supervising and feedback systems. If there is need to revisit problem areas do not make this the opening topic. Make sure that the criticism is valid and focused on actions, rather than on the person, and recognise any improvements since the previous discussion of the problem. If you have a staff member who is clearly unhappy or going through a difficult time the appraisal should be postponed and the underlying problems addressed. Never think to yourself, we can deal with that in appraisal. If it is praise, say it or do it immediately and keep appraisals as a shared review process.

Trouble shooting

If there is a failure to agree when the feedback given is refuted by the employee, a second interview should be set within two or three days to re-visit the areas of disagreement. If this interview fails to provide a solution a third party should be introduced as an arbiter and their decision is final.

Arbitration arrangements must be built into appraisals policy. The arbiter should be a named person to be called upon if there is an initial failure to agree.

Activity
Judy has been the practice receptionist for 30 years. She is set in her ways and cynical about CPD. She has made only minimal effort in terms of her development over a number of years. She was resistant when the appraisal system was introduced and the practice manager feels that Judy's participation in her appraisal is no more than paying 'lip-service'.

How should the practice manager manage Judy's appraisal?

The importance of trust and confidence

Without a basis of trust, appraisals will create apathy and disrespect. For an individual to truly participate in the appraisal process they must believe in the capabilities and integrity of the appraiser. To create trust the manager must:

- Follow practice policies
- Observe ethical codes
- Have delivered on previous promises.

Research shows that a failure in trust may be forgiven more easily if it is interpreted as a failure of competence rather than a lack of benevolence or honesty. The degree to which one party trusts another is a measure of belief in their honesty, fairness, or benevolence. Confidence is based upon a belief in the competence of another person and so for team members to have trust and confidence in the appraisals process requires a fair, consistent and structured process to be followed for each team member and that all actions agreed are honoured and followed through.

Staff training and **development policy**

When practices applied for Care Quality Commission (CQC) registration, many needed to dust off a series of random polices, previously collated and long forgotten. In many professional practices ethical intentions and high principles serve well in place of meaningful policy and procedures.

Policy and procedure

Once headline policy has been set in the business plan the role of the manager is to determine practical procedures for its implementation. These practical steps are the follow through between good intentions and practical results. In respect of a training and development policy, firstly you need to specify the aim or purpose of the policy and define the results that you expect to achieve through this policy. Then go on to make a clear statement in an opening to a policy statement, such as:

> 'Through our staff training and development activities we aim to safeguard the welfare of our patients and staff. Every member of the team will receive induction training and regular training updates to ensure full observation of legal and ethical guidelines'.

With this in place the next decision to be made is in respect of the scope of the policy, here you specify to which team members the policy is applicable. A staff development policy will apply universally to the entire team.

The next step is to identify the person accountable for the enforcement of the policy. This will ultimately be the employer, who may rely on the practice manager for the day-to-day implementation of the procedures; the practical measures selected to secure the policy's aims. The final section will be an outline of the review and monitoring processes, for example, this policy will be reviewed at least annually, or immediately if required.

Example Staff Development Policy

Purpose

This policy aims to provide a code of practice to underpin the highest standards of professionalism. The aim is to ensure our team are equipped to deliver the highest standards of patient care. This policy sets procedures and protocols to ensure that after achieving all required qualifications, staff maintain their knowledge and skills and update their learning to add value to the clinical and non-clinical patient care provided in this practice.

Scope

This policy applies to every member of the practice team. Each GDC registrant is required to meet the officially specified requirements, and those set in their personal development plan. Non registrants are required to complete the development targets in their personal development plan defined during their annual performance review. CPD must include relevant development of clinical, administrative, business and other skills as defined by the needs of the practice, set out in the business plan.

Accountability

The practice manager is responsible for monitoring training that has been completed. Each team member is responsible for recording their development activities and ensuring every reasonable effort is made to complete their agreed development plan.

Procedures

The practice has set a training budget to facilitate the aims of this policy. The following measures will be taken to ensure that the practice team continuously develop both interpersonal and professional skills.

1. New staff induction programme
2. Annual performance reviews
3. Job descriptions
4. Personal Development Plans
5. Mentoring
6. In house training sessions
7. Postgraduate training
8. Peer review
9. Membership of professionals associations

1 New staff induction programme

All new staff members are required to participate in our induction programme, 'Welcome to our Practice'. The greatest care is taken during staff selection to allow them to continuing their professional development throughout their career at this practice. During the three month induction programme new team members are given thorough training in health and safety requirements, the use of all materials, equipment, systems, policies and procedures. On completion of the induction programme a decision will be made whether to confirm the appointment with a permanent contract. This decision will be based upon a performance review at the end of the probationary period

2 Annual Performance Reviews (APR)

When a permanent contract has been accepted the first APR will take place, during which training and performance targets will be agreed up until the end of the current calendar year at which point they will join the practice APR system and the individual will be required to start building a CPD portfolio to be reviewed as part of their APR. This must contain:

- A current job description
- A Personal Development Plan
- CPD records
- Evaluations of activities carried out.

3 Job descriptions
All staff will be given a detailed job description upon recruitment. The aim of the job description is to outline work and team roles for each team member. Updates will be negotiated during APRs, in response to the development needs of the business and the team.

4 Personal Development Plans
All CPD activities endorsed by this practice must be consistent with GDC regulations and the overall aims of the practice. Training needs will be identified with reference to the following criteria:

- Legal requirements
- Ethical requirement
- Business development.

Agreed CPD activities aim to improve compliance/performance in at least one of the above areas. A learning contract, defining aims and objectives for the activity, will be established before any activity is 'signed off' by the practice manager.

5 Mentoring
This practice runs a mentoring system but this is *not intended to replace direct contact with the practice manager or directors*. The purpose of the system is to offer training opportunities and a first point of contact with the closest team member in terms of experience and background. Each member of the team will be appointed a mentor who will be able to offer guidance and support in respect of workplace issues. Confidentiality within this relationship will be respected within the scope of the practice code of conduct for mentoring. Any blatant breech of this code will be regarded as gross misconduct and could result in disciplinary action.

6 In- house training sessions
Monthly staff meetings will be held to a standard agenda. The meeting will include a training session on a topic relevant to the needs of the practice. Topics will include updates on Health and Safety issues and core CPD practical updates. Some of these sessions will be lead by team members and others will be lead by guest facilitators invited into the practice for their specialist knowledge. One month's notice of each session will be given to team members. Attendance at these sessions is required.

7 Postgraduate training
Where postgraduate training is required it is the responsibility of team members to fulfil their responsibilities. The practice will allocate time and in certain cases funding for travel and course fees, when at least four weeks' notice of attendance is given.

8 Peer review
In addition to monthly staff meetings, peer group meetings will be arranged within the practice. The purpose of these meetings is to audit performance and identify quality developments.

9 Membership of professionals associations
Employees are encouraged to join and actively participate in their professional associations. In certain cases, membership fees will be met from the CPD budget. Updates and development within groups of the profession should be discussed at staff meetings.

This policy will be reviewed at least annually, in conjunction with practice needs and professional requirements.

Training resources

Technology is revolutionising the way dental professionals' access training. In a practice survey 61% of DCPs viewed opportunities to complete CPD online, or through journals as a 'major advantage'. Practice managers may opt to oversee CPD activity by providing practice study sessions to include the following:

- Legal and ethical requirements
- The practice's policies
- Guidance on CPD planning and participation
- GDC guidelines.

Dental Practice Management

Linking CPD requirements to evidence

Activity	Competency Standard	Relevance	CPD Value	Funded by	General/ Verifiable
To attend the BDTA Dental Showcase Exhibition	1.4 To maintain currency	To gauge new developments & practices	4 hours	Practice	V
To read *Dental Nursing*, *Vital*, PPD	1.4 To maintain currency	To read articles and maintain currency	1 hour	Practice	G
BTEC Diploma in care coordination	3.1 To maintain theoretical aspects of dental nursing	To develop skills and gain a recognised qualification	120 hours Nominal learning	50% DCP 50% Practice	V
Staff meetings	1.4 To maintain currency	To focus on team and patient needs	1 hour	Practice	V
In house training sessions	1.4 To maintain currency	To maintain skills and knowledge	3 hours	Practice	V

Where the interest of the individual and the needs of the practice coincide through CPD there is real opportunity to ensure the aims of the practice are reinforced and supported. Practice policy should define where the practice will provide financial support for CPD activities.

Personal development should run alongside professional development because it is the key to the growth of confidence and motivation within the team. The happiness of the team is central to a successful business. Without the team on your side you can often feel as if you are fighting a losing battle; patients are acutely aware and can often comment if there is an 'atmosphere'. In this age of on-line customer reviews it is vital that a business provides its customers with every reason to write a glowing review.

Chapter 6:
Managing Employment Issues

This chapter looks at the background of employment law and considers contracts of employment, disciplinary and grievance procedures and the Equality Act 2010. As employment law is a rapidly evolving aspect of practice management this chapter looks at the underpinning principles, official bodies and broad themes. When required for policy building or taking remedial action, the finer detail should be gathered from your legal advisors, or from the range of government websites which will be introduced throughout this chapter. It is important to note that Scottish law can differ from English law. The information in this chapter applies to English law.

Glenys Bridges

The origins of **British employment law**

The origins of British law can be traced back to 1066 and the Norman Conquest when feudal barons used trial by ordeal techniques. Records show that in 1215 the Church intervened to stop this practice and introduced trial by jury. In the 1400s the legal system began to evolve its modern shape when of travelling judges on tours known as Assizes were introduced. In 1972 the Crown (criminal) and County (Civil) Courts Systems currently in place were introduced and in the 1970s the Tribunal system was introduced to make the law more accessible. When Britain joined the European Community, under the terms of the Treaty of Rome, we became subject to European Union (EU) rules and regulations and the authority of the European Court of Justice (ECJ), which legislates through:

- **Regulations**: Immediately binding upon member states
- **Directives**: Binding but member states choose how and when to introduce them
- **Decisions**: Binding on the state to which they directly apply.

Britain is subject to European Directives relating to Employment Law in respect of:

- Equal Pay
- Employee's Rights
- Health and Safety
- Freedom of movement for workers from member country to country
- Equality and Human Rights.

Enforcement

There are a number of bodies with responsible for enforcing employment law these are:

Employment Tribunals (ET)

The Tribunals system was set up in 1974 to deal with the majority of Employment Law actions. Tribunals make the law more accessible to the population in general hearing applications, sometimes called 'complaints' and appeals about employment matters such as:

Dental Practice Management

- Unfair dismissal
- Redundancy
- Equality
- Pay
- Terms and conditions of employment.

Tribunals are similar to courts in many ways, although less formal. Claims are heard by a Panel in the Employment Tribunal's offices. A tribunal panel generally has three members, the Chairman, who is legally qualified and appointed by the Lord Chancellor, plus two lay members appointed by the Secretary of State for Trade and Industry. They will be people with experience of resolving work related problems.

The time limits for Employment Tribunal are shorter than for the courts. Applications must be made within three months of the end of the employment, or from when the complaint occurred. Unlike in the courts, at Tribunals the parties cannot be ordered to pay costs for the other party, unless the tribunal considers that one party has behaved unreasonably.

County Courts

Civil (non criminal) cases are brought through the County Courts. This can include breach of contract, damages and wrongful dismissal cases. Anyone taking Employment Law action for claims in excess of £50K, or where damages need to be assessed the claim must apply to the County Court, where proceedings are more complicated and costly than in an Employment Tribunal.

Employment Relations Directorate (ERD)

Over recent years Employment Law has placed an increasing emphasis on social and political correctness. This has prompted guidance and directives from Europe and as a result the red tape with which businesses have needed to contend has increased. To help businesses work within the law the Government has created the Department for Business, Innovation and Skills to provide simplified information policy and legislation related to:

- European directives
- Representation in areas of employment rights
- Employment relations
- Hours of work

The ERD has operational responsibility for:

- Payment of redundancy and insolvency claims
- An employment agency standards inspectorate
- Monitoring on pay and advice on pay
- The arbitration service ACAS.

The ERD can be found on the government website bis.gov.uk formally berr.gov.uk

ACAS - Advisory, Conciliation and Arbitration Service

Founded in 1974, ACAS is a publicly funded body run by a council of 12 members from businesses, unions and the independent sector. ACAS employs about 800 people throughout England, Scotland and Wales and is structured into 11 main regions, plus a Head Office in London.

The Aim of ACAS is the prevention and resolution of problems in the workplace by:

- Providing telephone help lines providing free information to anyone with a work problem. This information is supported by an extensive range of publications and an informative website.
- Resolving problems. In 2001 93% of disputes involving ACAS were resolved.
- ACAS's focus remains on prevention and the promotion of good practice. The Advisory Service works with hundreds of companies every year to develop a joint approach to problem solving.
- Settling employee complaints. Over 100,000 each year apply to Employment Tribunals 71% of these are sorted out at pre- tribunal stages through ACAS.
- Education. ACAS run workshops and seminars on Employment Law subjects.

Employment contracts

The employment contract is central to employment law; a contract of employment is an agreement between employer and employee and forms the basis of the employment relationship. A contract of employment is an agreement between an employer and an employee setting out the rights and duties of both parties in the 'terms' of contract. The contract does not have to be in writing, but employees are entitled to a written statement of the main terms within two months of starting work.

Dental Practice Management

The contract is made as soon as a job offer is accepted, and both sides are then bound by its terms until it is properly ended (usually by giving notice) or, until the terms are changed (usually by mutual agreement).

Employment rights are dependent upon whether the employment status is classed as an 'employee', 'worker' or 'self employed'. This depends on the type of contract you have with your employer.

The contract of employment should specify:

- Date on which contract is given
- Names of parties
- Date of employment
- Wages - including overtime/calculation of bonuses
- Intervals at which wages will be paid
- Hours of work
- Holiday entitlement and what happens on leaving
- Job title and/or description
- Place of work
- Notice requirements.

In addition, information must be given about:

- Sick pay
- Pension scheme
- Duration of employment if temporary.

It is advisable for employment information to be supported by a staff handbook in which the relevant details are set out. The following information must be communicated to all staff members:

- Grievance and disciplinary procedure
- Reclaiming training costs
- Confidentiality
- Restrictive covenants
- Maternity leave
- Sickness policy

- Notification of absence and evidence of incapacity requirements
- Any other benefits.

In addition to the contract of employment it is also useful for the business to have a staff handbook which includes:

- Grievance and disciplinary procedures
- Arrangements for reclaiming of training costs, or not
- Defined standards for confidentiality
- Any restricted covenants agreed at the time of employment
- Arrangements for maternity leave
- Sickness policy - in-line with notification of absence and evidence of incapacity requirements
- Any other benefits the practice is allowing staff over and above its legal requirements.

There are many more additions which the handbook can contain, such as: equal opportunities policy, telephone protocols, complaints procedure and uniform requirements. The handbook should be tailor made to meet the businesses needs and must be clear, accessible and understood by all team members.

Disciplinary and Grievances Procedures

The ACAS Code of Practice
Disciplinary and Grievance Procedures

It is crucially important for this code to be followed: an employment tribunal will adjust any awards made by up to 25% for unreasonable failure to comply. Legislation setting out disciplinary and grievance procedures seeks to provide a clear and transparent framework for dealing with difficulties which can arise from either the employer's or employee's perspective. They standardise how everybody in similar circumstances is treated and ensure fair and reasonably interactions. Practice managers should consult and follow the ACAS Code of Practice for handling disciplinary and grievance issues as outlined below.

Disciplinary procedures are needed:
- So employees know what is expected of them in terms of standards of performance or conduct (and the likely consequences of continued failure to meet these standards)

Dental Practice Management

- To identify obstacles to individuals achieving the required standards (for example training needs, lack of clarity of job requirements, additional support needed) and take appropriate action
- As an opportunity to agree suitable goals and timescales for improvement in an individual's performance or conduct
- To try to resolve matters without recourse to an employment tribunal
- As a point of reference for an employment tribunal should someone make a complaint about the way they have been dismissed.

Grievance procedures are needed:
- To provide individuals with a course of action should they have a complaint (which they are unable to resolve through regular communication with their line manager)
- To provide points of contact and timescales to resolve issues of concern
- To try to resolve matters without recourse to an employment tribunal.

Disciplinary policy and practice

There are two main areas where a disciplinary system may be used: capability and performance, and conduct.

Capability/performance

Capability issues may arise because an employee does not have adequate training, or is unable to do the work to a satisfactory standard for another reason. An employer must try to identify the reason and give appropriate support, before taking disciplinary action.

An individual who is unable to do their job because of ill-health may also fall into this category. In these instances an employee should be dealt with sympathetically and offered support. However, unacceptable levels of absence could still result in the employer making use of warnings.

Conduct

Employee misconduct could range from continued lateness, failure to follow a reasonable management instruction, abuse of the organisation's computer system or Internet access, bullying behaviour or creating a hostile work environment, through to theft, fighting and committing criminal offences. The more grave offences may constitute gross misconduct. In all cases, an employer should follow the recommendations in the ACAS Code.

Stages of the process

If action is to be taken, it should observe at least the following three stages:

- Letter
- Meeting
- Appeal.

There must always be a full and fair investigation to determine the facts and to decide if further action is necessary. The ACAS Code recommends at least these three steps, however in some cases a second meeting stage may be appropriate.

When matters begin to escalate be sure to keep good records of all interactions, you will need to produce these records should a case be taken to an employment tribunal. Your records should include:

- All meetings minutes
- Emails
- Attendance notes
- Notes of telephone calls
- Copies of correspondence etc.

Disciplinary interviews

Managers should be trained and supported so that they are able to carry out disciplinary meetings which:

- Ensure all the facts are investigated in advance (including consulting the individual's personal file for relevant information) and plan how the meeting is to be approached
- Make sure the employee knows from the letter inviting them to the meeting why they have been asked to attend and that they have a right to have a companion present
- Make sure the individual has reasonable notice, ideally more than 72 hours, and that they have a chance to arrange an appropriate representative to attend if they wish
- Provide appropriate statements from people involved in advance of the meeting, together with any key information you intend to rely on
- Make sure another member of management can be there to take detailed notes and help conduct the interview

Dental Practice Management

- Never pre-judge the outcome of the interview before hearing the employee's perspective
- Start the interview by stating the complaint to the employee and referring to appropriate statements from people involved
- Give the employee ample opportunity to put forward their side of the story and call any supporting witnesses
- Employers can also call witnesses, but they can only be in the room for the relevant part of the interview, not the duration
- Make use of adjournments: always take a break to consider and obtain any extra information you need before reaching your decision. Adjournments can be useful if things become heated or people are upset during the interview
- Deliver the decision (and give reasons, taking into account any mitigating circumstances), confirm review periods and ensure you give details of how to appeal
- Confirm the decision in writing.

It is important that everyone involved in disciplinary action understand the importance of following the correct procedure, as even if the case against an employee seems proven, they can still be deemed to have been treated unfairly if the correct procedures are not followed.

Workers are entitled to be accompanied by a work colleague or trade union official at formal disciplinary and grievance interviews. It would be good practice for an employer to offer this at any investigatory meeting. Employers do not have to allow family members, or lawyers to accompany but can allow this if they wish.

Potential outcomes

No action – After the meeting, the employer may decide that no action is necessary. For example, if an employee was unclear about what was expected from them and they agree to try to resolve the issue via additional support or counselling.

Warnings – Alternatively, the employer may decide to give the employee a warning. An organisation's policy should outline exactly what warnings will be given, but the following are examples of warnings and organisation may use:

- Verbal/ oral warning (ACAS no longer recommends this stage as part of a formal procedure but, for cases of minor misconduct, this will often be a reasonable method to prevent a problem escalating)

- First written warning/improvement notice (PIP)
- Final written warning.

Employers should specific a 'life' for formal disciplinary warnings after which they are disregarded for disciplinary purposes. Typical timescales suggested in the A non statutory guidance for the types of warning are:

- First written warning – 6 months
- Final written warning – 1 year.

It may be appropriate for a warning to continue to be regarded for a longer period, provided the timescale was specified in the organisation's disciplinary policy from the outset. The time period employers select for warnings to remain current, and the penalties imposed, must be reasonable in all circumstances. For example, they must take into account the nature of the misconduct, the employee's disciplinary record and be consistent with penalties imposed in similar cases.

Dismissal

There are currently six potentially fair reasons for dismissal.

- Capability or qualifications
- Conduct
- Illegality or contravention of a statutory duty
- Some other substantial reason
- Redundancy
- Retirement - though this differs from the other potentially fair reasons for dismissal, regarding both the procedure and how 'fairness' is decided.

Employers need to be sure that any decision to dismiss an employee will be seen as 'reasonable' by an employment tribunal. The employer must follow the ACAS Code prior to any dismissal and also have been fair overall, for example by complying with internal procedures, treating employees consistently and carrying out a proper investigation.

Grievance policy and practice

It is essential that grievances from employees are treated in the same fair manner and that all practice managers are familiar with their organisation's grievance procedure.

Dental Practice Management

There are a number of additional factors to bear in mind when dealing with grievances concerning harassment.

In the Equality Act 2010 harassment is defined as: *"unwanted conduct related to a relevant protected characteristic, which has the purpose or effect of violating an individual's dignity or creating and intimidating, hostile, degrading, humiliating or offensive environment for that individual."*

Bullying is not specifically defined in law, but in their advice leaflet for employees, ACAS give the following definition: *"Bullying may be characterised as offensive, intimidating, malicious or insulting behaviour, an abuse or misuse of power through means intended to undermine, humiliate, denigrate or injure the recipient. Bullying or harassment may be by an individual against an individual (perhaps by someone in a position of authority such as a manager or supervisor) or involve groups of people. It may be obvious or it may be insidious."*

Harassment and bullying can range from extremes such as physical violence to less obvious forms like ignoring someone. They can be delivered in a variety of ways - with or without witnesses - and be persistent behaviour over a period of time, or a one-off act and can include:

- Physical contact which is unwanted
- Unwelcome remarks about a person's age, dress, appearance, race or marital status
- Jokes, offensive language, gossip, slander, sectarian songs and letters
- Posters, graffiti, obscene gestures, flags, bunting and emblems
- Isolation or non-cooperation and exclusion from social activities
- Coercion for sexual favours
- Pressure to participate in political/religious groups
- Intrusion by pestering, spying and stalking
- Failure to safeguard confidential information
- Shouting at staff
- Setting impossible deadlines
- Persistent criticism
- Personal insults.

Handling grievances informally

Individuals should be encouraged to discuss ordinary, day-to-day issues informally with their line manager. This helps concerns to be heard and responded to as soon as possible.

Handling grievances formally

Employees should also be aware of the formal route open to them, including:

- The three stages of the ACAS Code and any further elements of the organisation's additional procedures
- With whom to raise the complaint and appropriate sources of support
- Timescales within which the organisation will seek to deal with the complaint
- Details of the stages of the grievance procedure, for example, how a complaint may be raised with the next level of management if a satisfactory resolution is not reached.

An employee should be given the right to be accompanied to grievance hearings by a colleague or trade union representative as explained above. As in disciplinary matters, record keeping is important and the ACAS Code should be followed.

Disciplinary and grievance procedures are essential when informal mechanisms are ineffective, or where they are inappropriate given the nature of the issue arising. These procedures can also help prevent unnecessary staff turnover and absenteeism, as well as avoiding costly and time-consuming tribunal cases.

Rules

You can help avoid problems leading to Tribunals by agreeing company rules and drawing up workable procedures. Before drawing up a disciplinary procedure, consider what standards the procedure will be used to maintain, then set rules of conduct at work. The rules should be fair, reflect the needs of the organisation and be written in a way that everyone understands. When people know and accept the rules, they will be less likely to break them. Rules help ensure a consistency of management action and can improve efficiency. The rules should define requirements in respect of:

- Gross misconduct
- Timekeeping requirements
- Absence
- Holidays
- Health and safety
- Standards of work
- Personal appearance
- Use of company facilities

Dental Practice Management

- Smoking
- Equality.

It is counterproductive to have too many rules and advisable to consult with employees to avoid introducing rules that are unjustifiable and unlawful. Most disciplinary problems can be solved by informal discussions or counselling. However, if this fails to resolve the problem you will need a more formal approach.

A disciplinary procedure will:

- Encourage employees to achieve and maintain standards of behaviour
- Provide a fair and consistent method of dealing with alleged failures
- Remind managers and supervisors how disciplinary matters should be handled
- Minimise disagreements about disciplinary matters
- Reduce the need for dismissals.

What form should it take? The procedure should be tailored to your own needs, but it should:

- Be in writing
- Not discriminate on grounds of race, sex or disability, sexual orientation, religion or belief
- Specify to whom it applies
- Explain the penalties
- Deal with matters quickly
- Give workers the right to be accompanied (see above for information on the statutory right to be accompanied)
- Give employees the right to put their side of the case
- Specify who has the authority to take disciplinary actions
- Ensure that action is not taken without careful investigation
- Provide a right to appeal.

Equal opportunities

On 1 October 2010, significant changes with implications for dental practices as both employers and service providers, were introduced in the Equality Act 2010. Under this

Act all employers and providers of goods or services to the public need to accommodate significant changes. The Act seeks to streamline and combine previous legislation and make things easier for businesses. The Act aims to protect minority groups from being discriminated against by clarifying 'protected characteristics'. Whilst this is beneficial for society as a whole, in reality this legislation will hit small businesses hard at the very time when they not only are fighting for survival due to the financial down turn, but are drowning in a sea of red tape.

One of the key changes is the clarification of Protected Characteristics consists of an expanded list of grounds for bringing discrimination claims as follows:

- Age
- Disability (including mental health and people diagnosed as clinically obese),
- Race
- Religion or beliefs
- Sexual orientation
- Gender reassignment (people who are having or who have had a sex change, transvestites and transgender people)
- Marriage and civil partnership
- Pregnancy and maternity.

Having defined the target groups the Act sets out to protect, it goes on to define seven different types of discrimination as follows:

- **Direct discrimination**: discrimination because of a protected characteristic
- Associative discrimination: direct discrimination against someone because they are associated with another person with a protected characteristic. (This includes carers of disabled people and elderly relatives, who can claim they were treated unfairly because of duties that they had to carry out at home relating to their care work. It also covers discrimination against someone because, for example, their partner is from another country)
- **Indirect discrimination**: when you have a rule or policy that applies to everyone but disadvantages a person with a protected characteristic.
- **Harassment**: there are many important aspects to the Act; however the area that needs to be highlighted is the expanded range and definitions of harassment as behaviour deemed offensive by the recipient. Employees can claim they find something offensive even when it is not directed at them. Employers are potentially

liable for the harassment of staff or customers by people they don't directly employ, such as a contractor or people visiting their premises, under the 'harassment by a third party' rule. It means you could be held responsible if a customer on your premises tells racist jokes. How this liability will work in practice, and how hard the tribunal courts will come down on business owners in this unfortunate situation through no fault of their own remains to be seen. The definition of harassment now means an employee who simply overhears an offensive comment, even if it is not directed at them, can hold you legally responsible for it. Managers need to make sure everyone in their team understands the rules and implications.

- **Victimisation**: discrimination against someone because they made or supported a complaint under Equality Act legislation.
- **Discrimination by perception**: direct discrimination against someone because others think they have a protected characteristic (even if they do not).

On a practical level it is important to note that you can no longer ask a prospective employee about their health before making a job offer, unless you can prove you are checking whether the employee would be able to carry out an essential task, or for the purpose of monitoring diversity. You can screen health once you have made a job offer - but then of course you would be opening a whole new can of worms if you rescind your job offer on the grounds of a disability, as you are then liable to be taken to tribunal too. 'Health' means physical disabilities and mental health problems. This also means you can't ask how much time an employee has taken off work in their previous jobs in an interview.

You can't treat someone unfavourably because of something connected to a disability e.g. spelling mistakes because of dyslexia. Disabled people can now claim any rule or requirement which disadvantages people with a certain disability as being indirect discrimination.

Mothers are allowed to breastfeed in public (on premises) - they can't be asked to go to a more private place.

Age is still the only protected characteristic by which you can justify direct discrimination, because you can argue that treating someone differently because of their age is allowed as long as it means you are doing it to meet a legitimate aim. You can also still have a default retirement age of 65 (unless/until the retirement age legislation changes, which it may do in the coming years).

People making claims can now bring a 'dual discrimination' claim, meaning the tribunal assesses the impact of the two protected characteristics in conjunction (for example, 'young Polish') where before they considered each protected characteristic separately ('young' and 'Polish') - which often didn't reveal the full extent of the discrimination, as discrimination on two grounds is often worse than just one. However, only two characteristics can be combined, no more. Dual discrimination will strengthen claims that were previously made for only one protected characteristic.

Actively promoting equality, diversity and human rights at your practice for staff and patients

Providing fair and accessible care and employment should be a strategic objective. With this underpinning philosophy, you will logically follow through measures that respect equality, diversity and human rights such as the following practical measures:

- Adapt practice premises to include an accessible, well lit and well signed entrance, emergency exit signs and elimination of steps with flush doorways or ramps wherever the physical structure of the building allows this
- Provision of hearing loops for patients with sensory impairment
- Access to translation services when needed
- A disabled entrance ramp and access to a treatment room as well as an accessible toilet for wheelchair users or, for wheelchair users we have mitigated restrictions to physical access at our own premises by establishing a referral system to another local practice which has offers wheelchair access
- Displaying a Practice Philosophy statement such as: "We build our services to respond effectively and efficiently to patients' needs. Our priority is to promote equality, diversity and human rights, to this end our team has been trained to take all reasonable actions to cater for patients with specific needs, including those with disabilities they will:
  – Interact comfortably with all people
  – Never patronise, or assume that they know best
  – Offer assistance but not impose it
  – Ask whether patients have a specific requirement and provide a sensible response
  – Ensure conversations with young, or disabled people are carried out at their eye-level
  – Offer a seat or help with the doors

- Offer their arm for guidance and support if required
- Adapt means of communication to ensure effective message delivery
- Talk to the patient directly and not solely through their companion
- Respect the patient's privacy and confidentiality, and never compromise this right
- Ask our patients about their particular requirements in advance incorporating a standard line in letters or as part of our customer care procedure (e.g. 'Please let us know if you require any particular assistance…')
- Incorporate requests for adjustments into our practice procedures
- Include a system of recording new or unmet requests and for considering how to deal with them in a timely manner."

Under the section 2 requirements for Care Quality Commission (CQC) registration, practices must ensure they have formal polices in place to shape their services and accommodate the needs of all of their patients. To this end practices need to have a disability policy in place and to record patient's ethnicity, so that services can be designed to meet the needs of the practice's population. This information can then be used to develop and deliver bespoke equality training covering all permitted characteristics to the dental team.

The Employment Relations Directorate (ERD) - is available on-line at: *www.berr.gov.uk*

Further reading
- The Employment Act 2008
- The Employment Tribunals (Constitution and Rules of Procedure) (Amendment) Regulations 2008 *http://www.cipd.co.uk/subjects/hrpract/absence/absncman.htm*

References

Books, reports and online
- ACAS (2009). *Disciplinary and grievance procedures*. Code of Practice 1. London: Acas. Available at: http://www.acas.org.uk/CHttpHandler.ashx?id=1047
- ACAS (2009). *Discipline and grievances at work*. London: Acas. Available at: http://www.acas.org.uk
- Department for Business Innovation and Skills (2009). *Avoiding and resolving discipline and grievance issues at work*. London: BIS. Available at: http://www.cipd.co.uk/subjects/emplaw/discipline/_dscgrvwrk.htm
- Incomes Data Services (2009). *Discipline, grievance and mediation*. HR Studies. London: IDS.

- Macdonald LAC (2010). *Managing discipline*. Kingston upon Thames: Wolters Kluwer.
- Parkin M (2009). *The employer's guide to grievance & discipline procedures: identifying, addressing and investigating employee misconduct*. London: Kogan Page.

Journals

- Acas Code of Practice on disciplinary and grievance procedures: Q&A. (2009) *IDS Employment Law Brief*. February. pp14-18.
- Disciplinary proceedings - an update. (2010) *IDS Employment Law Brief*. No 906, August. pp14-18.
- Newman D (2010). Conflicting events. *Employers' Law*. July. pp18-19.
- Payne R (2007). *How to conduct an effective internal investigation. People Management*. 13: No 20, 4 October. pp42-43.
- Suff R (2010). IRS 2010 dispute resolution survey: grievances and the new Acas code of practice. *IRS Employment Review*. 12 April, 8pp.
- Suff R (2010). IRS 2010 dispute resolution survey: managing discipline. *IRS Employment Review*. 26 April, 10pp.

Chapter 7:
Promoting a Healthy Workplace

This chapter covers the background and origins of the legal codes related to health and wellbeing in the modern dental workplace environment. It outlines legal responsibilities, the role of the enforcement agencies and shows how legal requirements can be implemented in dental businesses so as to benefit all those affected by the work of the practice. Health and Safety law is ever evolving and so this chapter will focus and the broad principles and management of health and safety rather than the finer detail of current requirements, which can be found on the Health and Safety Executive's website *www.hse.gov*

An important part of the Health and Safety Executive's (HSE) role is to help businesses meet occupational health and safety requirements. The HSE implement changes arising from the UK parliament on two common commencements these being 6th April and 1st October each year. When possible any changes in European law are also introduced.

Origins of UK safety legislation

The earliest health and safety law was the Factories Act 1802. This legislation addressed issues related to welfare, control of working hours and provision of rest rooms to place limitations on the employment of minors and women, as well as to address safety issues. By the 1960s health and safety law was spread over nine main sets of legislation, administered by five government departments, through seven independent inspectorates. This made the law complex and inaccessible to ordinary people, to address this the Robens Committee was appointed to consider how to make this area of the law more effective.

In 1972 The Robens Committee reported three main concerns:

- New technology and the increases in the scale of industrial operations had increased workplace hazards with which legislation had failed to keep up
- The existing regulations only set rules to be followed in specified situations; this had made the law complicated and patchy, covering some industries and omitting others
- Legislation did little to encourage employers to improve conditions beyond the rules laid down in the regulations.

The Robens Committee concluded that these matters could be rectified by placing a strong emphasis on self-regulation and communication between employers and employees. They recommended the introduction of the formal statements of safety policy and the use of systematic hazard assessments which are in place today. They also recommended the unification of all enforcing bodies under one executive. This was enacted in the Health and Safety at Work Act of 1974.

The Health and Safety at Work etc Act (1974) HSAWA

In 1974 the HSAWA was introduced and for the first time health and safety law applied to anyone affected by work activities, and so brought 5 million workers not previously covered under its protection. It was a consolidation of all the previous legislation with regulations and approved codes of conduct. The HSAWA is an 'enabling' Act, which means that it provides an umbrella under which regulations to cover specific areas are encompassed. An important feature of the Act is that it imposes a duty of care upon employers, employees, the self-employed, manufacturers and suppliers as follows:

Employers

Are required as far as reasonably practicable, to safeguard the health safety and welfare of their workforce. This is a re-statement of a pre existing duty of care under civil law. In particular they are required to provide:
- Provide safe system of work and safe plant.
- Issue a Statement of Safety Policy and bring it to the attention of the workforce
- Inform employees on safety matters on a right to know basis
- Train employees in safe practices
- Besides employees, employers have a similar duty to others including contractors and the general public

Employees

The responsibilities of employees are to:
- Take reasonable care of him or her self and others
- Co-operate with the employer in safety matters

Manufacturers/Suppliers

Must ensure that:
- Any substance, or article provided is safe when used properly
- Instructions are provided to allow safe usage of their products.

European Directives

The HSAWA Act is widely considered to have modernised safety law by allocating general duties on all persons involved in work activities. As a member of the European Community, the UK is subject both to UK statutory law and European Directives.

One of the most important EU directives for health and safety is a group of six Regulations commonly known as the 'Six Pack'. These directives are concerned with the management of workplace health and safety, across all the European States, The 'six pack' was adopted by the UK in 1992 and came into effect on 1 January 1993. It consists of the following regulations:

- The Management of Health and Safety at Work Regulations 1992 (amended 1999)
- The Workplace (Health, Safety and Welfare) Regulations 1992
- The Provision and Use of Work Equipment Regulations 1992 (amended 1998)
- The Manual Handling Operations Regulations 1992
- The Health and Safety (Display Screen Equipment) Regulations 1992
- The Personal Protective Equipment at Work Regulations 1992.

Updated in 1999 these regulations cover: heating, lighting and ventilation at work; the safe use of computer screens and keyboards; handling heavy or awkward loads; rest breaks; and personal protective equipment. Regulation 3, places a legal duty on employers to carry out a series of risk assessments as a first step to ensuring workplace safety, this activity lies at the heart of a modern approach to health and safety at work.

Enforcement of Health and Safety Regulations

The Health and Safety Executive enforces Health and Safety law. Their inspectors have a right of access to inspect any workplace and can take the following actions if the Act is being contravened:

Seizure

To enforce the HSWA, inspectors may enter work premises in which they have cause to believe dangerous work situation exist. If they have reasonable cause to expect serious obstruction, they may take a police officer and seize and make harmless (by destruction if necessary) any article or substance which they have reasonable cause to believe is a cause of imminent danger of serious personal injury.

Improvement Notice

Health and Safety Inspectors use Improvement Notices where there is no serious risk, but there is a breach of legislation. An Improvement Notice allows a period of time for improvements to plant, equipment, processes, etc. to be carried out. If improvements are not completed within the specified time, the employer is in breach of the Notice, and consequently in breach of the Act. If a recipient of the Notice is aggrieved by the conditions of the Notice, they have the right of appeal to an Industrial Tribunal. The appeal should be lodged within 21 days of the date of the Notice. A copy of the standard appeal form is always issued with the Notice.

Prohibition Notice

Inspectors can use prohibition notices to stop any process, activity or the use of machinery which involves, or will involve risk to health, or serious personal injury. Prohibition Notices may either come into effect immediately if the risk is imminent, or alternatively be deferred.

Prosecution

Initially, inspectors will offer advice and guidance to help employers meet their legal duties. They would only decide to prosecute if there is enough evidence and if prosecution is in the public interest. Prosecution is likely when:

- Someone has been **killed** due to a breach of law
- The offence or injury is serious, or the general approach of the offender warrants it
- There has been **repeated** poor compliance
- The standard of safety management falls far below that expected and causes significant risk
- There has been a **failure to comply** with an improvement notice or prohibition notice
- There has been an intent to **deceive** in relation to a matter which gives rise to significant risk
- Inspectors have been intentionally **obstructed** in the course of their duties.

The maximum penalty possible under health and safety legislation depends on the offence.

Understanding Health and Safety

To effectively manage health and safety at work we need to define the requirements for safe working environments, this will include:

- Clean working environments
- A mutual duty of care
- Ergonomically aware staff
- Risk assessments
- Risk reduction measures implemented
- Hazards removed or managed.

A safe working environment is one in which accident prevention measures have been addressed when 'accident' is defined as:

- Unplanned events resulting in injury for example: cuts, bruises, fractures, burns
- Something that happens due to human error
- Unforeseeable events that could not have been prevented
- Undesired occurrences resulting in emotional or physical harm
- Uncontrolled situation that results in harm to a person.

The Domino Theory

A risk management approach looks at the sequence of events that led to the accident resulting in injury, loss or damage. This is commonly referred to as the Domino Theory of accident causation. This theory was introduced by Heinrich in the 1920's. Heinrich's Domino Theory suggests that an accident leading to injury or damage is the result of a five stage sequence and each stage (domino) represents a linked cause. Remove any one and the sequence cannot run its course and the accident will be prevented. The five stages are:

1. Work situation
2. Fault of person
3. Unsafe act
4. Accident
5. Injury or damage.

There are thousands of accidents in the workplace every year and it has been estimated that in Britain alone 2.5 million people suffer work-related ill health. Accidents and illness cause a great deal of personal pain and suffering for individuals, as well as financial difficulty for families. Employers have to provide temporary cover during staff absence and can lose money as a result of disrupted business. While there are direct costs involved in developing good health and safety standards at work, such as investment in training and new equipment, there are also huge long-term savings that can benefit individuals, families and companies.

Health and safety management

Health and safety management is no different from other forms of management, in order for it to be effective it needs to be structured and tangible. In small organisations, such as dental practices, the pressures of running the business can overrun health and safety considerations. However it is vital to realise that enforcing officers and insurance companies are increasingly looking for evidence of effective health and safety management in workplaces.

Employers are required to identify and determine strategies tailored to their own workplaces. This requires them to apply five key principles of effective management. The key principles to successful health and safety management require the manager to:

1. **Set policy**
All businesses must have a Health and Safety policy, although it need only be in writing when the company employs five or more people. The purpose of the policy is to promote a positive health and safety culture.

A full Health and Safety policy will be a substantial document. To ensure that the most essential safety measures are universally communicated a Statement of Essential Health and Safety, which will be a much shorter document, should be made available. This will open with an undertaking to comply with all relevant legislation, then go on to defines responsibilities throughout the dental team, identify relevant safe working practices and policy review processes.

2. **Plan policy implementation**
Implementation of health and safety measures should involve the whole team. Each person should be aware of their role in securing a range of measurable and achievable objectives. Risk assessments must be conducted to provide basic information on the current situation so that the manager can identify and prioritise needs and determine suitable controls.

3. **Organise staff training**
All team members need to know how to meet their health and safety responsibilities. Clear lines and methods of reporting must be established and effective communication methods for health and safety defined. A valuable approach to team health and safety training can be found in the 4 C's approach as follows:

- **Competence** – staff must have the necessary skills, training, knowledge and experience to carry out tasks safely
- **Control** – defined health and safety responsibilities throughout all levels of the organisation
- **Co-operation** – throughout all levels of the organisation develops a positive health and safety culture
- **Communication** – effective communication throughout all levels, verbal, written and visible.

4. **Monitor performance**
With clear objectives in place and communicated, the next step is to measure and monitor the results they achieve. When quality audit principles are applied to the results achieved it is possible to assess the effectiveness and efficiency of the outcomes and make necessary adjustments.

- *Reactive monitoring systems* measure failure for example: accident figures, sickness records, damage to property and equipment.
- *Proactive monitoring systems* measure achievement and compliance e.g. inspections, comparisons against projected performance, review and revision of objectives.

5. **Audit and review**
Auditing measures overall success of the policy and establishes the level of compliance. A regular, planned review of policy is needed to meet legal and operational needs. Change is constant and inevitable so audit and review processes are required to ensure systems and their implementation remain valid and relevant. The most effective audit and review systems are those which include all interested parties and where consultation takes place prior to any revisions being made.

Health and Safety Policy

Good health and safety standards bring benefits for individuals and practices. There are two equally important reasons to have a health and safety policy, those being legal obligations and practical management reasons.

Legal obligations

The Health and Safety at Work Act 1974 requires employers, who employ five or more people, to prepare and, as often as may be appropriate, revise their written health and safety policy, and to bring the statement and any revisions to the notice of all employees.

The Management of Health and Safety at Work Regulations 1999, requires employers to arrange for the effective planning, organisation, control, monitoring and review of health and safety measures. Where five or more are employed these must be documented.

The Health and Safety (Consultation with Employees) Regulations 1996, requires employers to consult with employees when health and safety arrangements are formulated, implemented, monitored and reviewed.

Practical management

It is important to distinguish between a health and safety policy and a practice safety manual, these are not the same, but are often combined. The policy must be user friendly and a 'live' working aide memoir. The most senior partner should sign the statement and date it and an issue or version number is useful when revising the policy. It should also outline employees' general commitments.

A policy generally comprises of three parts:
- A statement of commitment
- Designation of responsibilities
- Arrangements for carrying out the policy.

A statement of commitment – should include commitments to:
- Safeguard the health and safety of all persons
- Comply with health and safety legislation relevant to the work activities
- Inform, instruct and train the team

- Make managers responsibility for supervising work
- Make arrangements for consultation with the team
- Monitor, review and revise where appropriate.

Designation of responsibilities includes the following tasks:
- Structure and responsibilities for implementing health and safety at all levels
- Establishes a clear line of communication
- Precise duties must be set out for everyone
- Names, job titles and functions for employees who are given additional health and safety duties
- Employers must appoint a competent person, to assist in managing the policy
- Job descriptions must reflect responsibilities
- Responsibilities must be measured and evaluated, this is accountability
- Responsibilities must be effectively designated; individuals must have experience, knowledge, training and skills to carry out their duties.

Arrangements for carrying out the policy:
- Specifies methods and measures for ensuring health and safety
- Each page should be numbered and dated for revision purposes
- Tailored to the individual needs or the practice
- Covers all eventualities
- Supported by working procedures.

Practical Management – Model Health and **Safety Statement**

> Our policy is to provide and maintain safe and healthy working conditions, equipment and systems of work for all our employees and to provide the training and supervision required for this purpose. The practice will take all reasonable steps to maintain premises, equipment and work systems so that they are safe and without risk to health. All appropriate regulations and codes of practice will be observed. Employees also have a responsibility to take care of the health and safety of themselves and others.
>
> ### Responsibilities
> The practice principal is responsible for health and safety in the practice, all

Dental Practice Management

incidents and spillages and training staff in health and safety matters. All incidents and events should be reported in the first instance to the practice manager and you should ask the practice manager for help it you are in any doubt about using materials or equipment.

Accidents
Report all accidents (including spillages and sharps injuries etc.) immediately, whether or not they involve personal injury. Ensure accidents are recorded in the accident book and all sections are completed. The practice First Aid box is clearly marked and is kept in _____ .

General fire safety
The fire extinguishers and alarms are regularly maintained and tested. Extinguishers are located _____ . Training in the use of these appliances is given to all staff.

Hygiene
It is the responsibility of all team members to maintain rigorous personal hygiene. Surgery staff must wear surgical gloves before handling instruments and materials to be used in the mouth. All substances that have been in contact with the mouth must be assumed to be contaminated and either sterilised or disposed of as instructed. Contaminated needles and sharps are to be disposed of in designated containers; heavy duty gloves must be worn when handling them and every precaution taken to avoid injury.

Hazards
All substances used in the practice must be handled carefully and care taken to avoid skin contamination, inhalation or ingestion.

Personal protection
Full use must be made of clothing, masks, gloves and glasses provided.

Manual handling
Lifting or moving a heavy object has the potential to cause injury unless care is taken. The protocol on manual handling procedures should be studied and adhered to.

Electrical equipment
Electrical equipment must NEVER be touched with wet hands. In the event of a malfunction, disconnect at the mains and affix a label stating that the machine is 'OUT OF ORDER'

Machinery
Never use any machinery unless you have been instructed in its safe use; make no attempt to dismantle, repair or service machinery without instruction.

Pressure vessels
Compressors and autoclaves are pressure vessels and must only be operated by team members who have been fully trained in their safe use. All compressors and autoclaves are regularly inspected, serviced and certified.

Control of substances hazardous to health (COSHH)
The practice complies with the COSHH regulations 2002. All staff should be familiar with the practice's COSHH documentation which is kept in the office. Training is provided and regularly updated. All team members are required to sign the COSHH documents to confirm that they have received training.

Radiography
The practice complies with the Ionising Radiation Regulations 1999 and Ionising Radiation (medical exposure) Regulations 2000. These regulations are for the protection of staff, patients and the public. All radiographic equipment must be operated in accordance with local rules which are to be found next to each machine. Appropriate training in radiological protection will be given to all staff; however, only those staff with appropriate training as specified in the regulations may actually take radiographs.

Manage pressure at work
We recognise that from time to time all team members, including dentists, feel under pressure, whether arising from work or domestic responsibilities. Do make these situations known as we may be able to help.

Food and drink
Beverages are acceptable in surgeries as long as they are in non-clinical areas or on reception and as long as they are discreet and tidy. Food, however, must

Dental Practice Management

NEVER be taken into the surgeries and may only be consumed in the staff room.

Medical conditions
You should inform the practice manager if you suffer from any medical condition which may require extra care by the practice, particularly in an emergency. Any information given will be treated in the strictest confidence.

Resuscitation in emergency
All team members must attend regular training in resuscitation techniques and procedures. These sessions are organised by the practice and will take place during normal working hours in conjunction with the practice manager. The portable oxygen cylinder is in _____ . Other resuscitation equipment is also kept in _____ , as is the emergency drug kit. The drug kit is always unlocked when the practice is working, but locked away when there is no one on the premises. An emergency collapse procedure is displayed in the reception area.

Review of Health and Safety Policy
Our practice Health and Safety Policy will be kept up to date, particularly when the practice introduces new material and equipment. To ensure this, the policy and the way in which it is operated will be reviewed every year and practice meetings will be held regularly to discuss any interim problems.

Signed _____ on behalf of the practice

_____ on behalf of the employee

Dated _____

Organisations that have the most successful health and safety records are those that integrate health and safety into their general management principles.

Having a policy is only the beginning. Management of health and safety requires that the acts and omissions of all people do not put their own or other people's safety at risk. Here you will state all measures taken to ensure that all people on practice premises are aware of, and comply with, your health and safety policy. This answer should explain the Duty of Care and show how you as an employer have taken adequate measures to make the work environment safe.

Circulation and distribution of the policy

Creating a valid policy is the beginning of the essential communication between employer and employee which is required for the policy to achieve its objectives.

Communicating health and safety measures

This process begins before the commencement of employment; as part of the induction process the new employee should be given the practice statement of health and safety. On their first day the contents should be discussed, practical aspects built into the initial training programme and the employee asked to sign to confirm that this has taken place.

The contract of employment and job description should specify tasks and requirements for health and safety compliance. In this way standards of behaviour can be set and monitored as part of the appraisals process.

Health and safety issues should have a regular slot in staff meeting agendas. The aim being to provide opportunities to introduce new regulations and to explore events, such as any near miss situations that may have occurred to ensure that timely remedial actions are taken. To demonstrate that corrective action is taken following incidents or near misses, an action plan should be produced to set targets and procedures.

Employers have a legal duty under the Health and Safety Information for Employees Regulations (HSIER) to display the approved poster in a prominent position in each workplace or to provide each worker with a copy of the approved leaflet outlining British health and safety law. The 2009 poster replaced the April 1999 version. The 2009 version was redesigned to be more readable and engaging to make health and safety information more accessible.

The Reporting of Injuries, Diseases and Dangerous Occurrences Regulations 1995 (RIDDOR), require you to report work-related accidents, diseases and near-miss incidents. Reports can now be made on-line or by telephone, full details and on line forms are available on the HSE website but health and safety education relies mainly on good communication, and consultation with employees on health and safety

Dental Practice Management

matters can be very important in creating and maintaining a safe and healthy working environment. Through consultation, your practice can motivate the workforce and increase awareness of health and safety issues, and in turn your operations should become more efficient with a reduced number of accidents and work-related illnesses.

Risk assessment

Under the Management of Health and Safety Regulations factors that place workers at risk of injury, or violence in the workplace must be identified and controlled as part of the employers Duty of Care. Dental employers should carry out and record risk assessments for the following work activities and environments:

- Autoclaves
- Children
- COSHH
- Cross infection control
- Display screens regulations
- Electricity
- Emergency drugs and equipment
- Ergonomics
- Fire
- First aid
- Staff training
- Iodising regulations
- Lone workers
- Noise
- Personal protective equipment (PPE)
- Nursing and pregnant mothers
- Sharps
- Slips, trips and falls
- Stress
- Smoking
- Vaccinations
- Violence to staff
- Young people
- Waste
- Water
- Working equipment

Prevention

A number of environmental, administrative and behavioural strategies can potentially reduce the risk of workplace violence. Examples of prevention strategies include:

- Good visibility within and outside the workplace
- Cash handling policies
- Physical separation of workers from customers or clients
- Good lighting
- Security devices

Promoting a Healthy Workplace   127

- Employee training.

All employees and employers should assess the risk of violence in their workplaces and take appropriate action to reduce those risks. A workplace violence prevention programme should include a system for documenting incidents, procedures to be taken in the event of incidents, and open communication between employers and employees.

Completing risk assessments

To ensure that you have taken the required steps to assess and reduce all risks relevant to the reception area complete a risk assessment form for each aspect, activity and area of the practice. Examples include:

- Lay out of reception area
- Cash handling processes
- Staff clothing
- Public access to your premises
- Method of raising the alarm if necessary.

You should complete a form for each aspect of your reception area.

Stress and wellbeing – workplace stress

Many in practice teams find that covering for staff sickness is one of their foremost challenges. Most of them have experienced the added pressure placed upon them when colleagues are absent from work and that to some degree it has been detrimental to their own well being.

In many small workplaces the 'S' word is something of a taboo, this is quite possibly because of the sense of powerlessness it encapsulates. The Health and Safety Executive (HSE) define stress as *"The adverse reaction people have when excessive pressure or other types of demands are placed upon them".* It is important then to make a distinction between pressures, which managed correctly can promote enthusiasm, energy and well being and stress which occurs when pressure is so excessive or prolonged that it outstrips the individual's coping mechanisms and results in deteriorating physical and mental health.

Dental Practice Management

Research commissioned by the HSE indicated that:

- Work-related stress accounts for over a third of all new incidences of ill health
- Each case of work-related stress, depression or anxiety related ill health leads to an average of 30.2 working days lost
- In 2009/10 an estimated prevalence of 435,000 people in Great Britain, who worked in the previous year, suffered from stress caused or made worse by their current or past work. This equates to 1,500 per 100,000 people (1.5%)
- An absence management survey report found stress-related absence is increasing and that stress is:
  - One of the most important reasons behind sickness from work
  - The cause of more staff absences than the common cold.

The recent trend toward companies downsizing for cost reduction or outsourcing has lead to longer working hours, job insecurity, and a conflict between the demands of home and work. As a result:

- 42% of managers feel illness rates in their organisation have gone up over the last 12 months
- 33% of workers claim a culture of not taking time off work for sickness exists in their organisation
- Only 53% feel they would be treated sympathetically if they were ill.

These survey results are concerning since in 2000, the Health and Safety Commission (HSE) identified stress as one of eight priority programmes for reducing ill health in the workplace; and in working in conjunction with the Department of the Environment, Transport and the Regions (DETR) launched the Revitalizing Health and Safety initiative to manage work-related stress through a range of actions including the introduction of management standards for tackling work-related stress and target action where it is most needed. The fact that more than 10 years later the situation has worsened indicates that it is time to go beyond management standards to break the power of the type of urban myths linked to stress that force people into denial reactions arising from beliefs such as:

- Stress is a sign of weakness
- It is best to carry on regardless
- Only neurotics become stressed.

Having accepted that it is OK to feel stressed, it becomes possible to find ways to raise your stress tolerance levels by:

- **Establishing support networks** – a strong network of supportive friends and family members is an enormous buffer against life's stressors. Lonely and isolated people are most vulnerability to stress
- **Develop a sense of control** – confidence in yourself and your ability to influence events and persevere through challenges makes it easier to take stress in one's stride. People who are vulnerable to stress tend to feel that things are out of their control
- **Positive mental attitude** – stress-hardy people have an optimistic attitude. They tend to embrace challenges, have a strong sense of humour, accept that change is a part of life, and believe in a higher power or purpose
- **Emotional Intelligence** – the ability to bring your emotions into balance helps people to bounce back from adversity
- **Knowledge and preparation** – the more you know about a stressful situation, including how long it will last and what to expect, the easier it is to cope. For example, if you go into surgery with a realistic picture of what to expect post-op, a painful recovery will be less traumatic than if you were expecting to bounce back immediately

We all too often have very little control over many of the events and circumstances that make us feel stressed. Stress is such a personal experience and its affects are so individual that acknowledging how it affects your team and building a strong supportive team culture is ultimately the way to reduce the stress cycle at work.

Additional Information

Bibliography

- Basic Guide to Medical Emergencies in the Dental Practice (Blackwell), Phil Jevon. 978-1-4051-9784-7.
- ACAS Code of Good Practice, (HMSO).
- BDA Compendium (BDA).
- Dental Reception and Practice Management (Blackwell), Glenys Bridges. 1-4051-3888-2.
- How to Manage (Butterworth–Heinemann), Ray Wild. CN6275.
- Increase Productivity, Profits and your own Prosperity (Fontana Collins), Blanchard and Johnson. 0-00636753-4.
- Management of Health and Safety in Dental Practice (Blackwell), Jane Bonehill. 1-40518-5929.
- Management Theory and Practice (DP Publications), G.A. Cole. 1-85805-166-5.
- Managing Budgets (Dorling Kindersley), Stephen Brookson. 0-7513-0771-8.
- Motivation to Work (Staples Press), Fred Hertzberg. 10-156000634x.
- Practice of Management (Heinemann), Peter Drucker. 978-0-7506-8504-7.
- Scientific Management (Harper Row), Fredrick .W Taylor. 978--14346-3820-5.
- Standards for Dental Professionals (General Dental Council).
- The Managers Handbook (Warner Books), Ernst and Young. 0-7515-1414-4.
- The Seven Habits of Highly Effective People (Simon Schuster), Stephen Covey. 0-671-71117-2.
- Transforming Company Culture (McGraw Hill), David Drenning. 0-07-707660-5.

Dental Practice Management

Recommended Reading

- 20th Century Mavericks (20th Century Fax), Britto Crow. 10-0953645401.
- Emotional Intelligence (Bloomsbury), Daniel Goleman. 0-7474-53984-7.
- Empowerment takes more than a minute (Berrett-Koehler), Ken Blanchard. 1-881052-83-4.
- Farther Reaches of Human Nature (Penguin), Abraham Maslow. 01-40042652.
- Helping Patients To Say Yes (Stephen Hancocks Ltd), Newsome and Latter. 978-0-9546145-7-7.
- How to Run a Successful meeting in half the time (Corgi Books), Milo O. Frank. 0-552-13615-8.
- Measuring Business Performance (Chartered Institute of Management Accountants), Mick Broadbent. 0-7494-3055-9.
- Psychological Testing for Managers (Piatkus), Stephanie Jones. 0-7499-1297-9.
- Quality Management System (Industrial Press), Walter Willborn. 0-8311-3013-X.
- The 5 temptations of a manager (Vermilion), Patrick Lencioni. 0-09-181960-1.
- The Age of Unreason (Arrow Books), Charles Handy. 0-09-975740-0.
- The Empty Raincoat (Arrow Books), Charles Handy. 0-09-930125-3.
- The Psychology of Dental Patient Care (BDJ Books), Ruth Freeman. 0-90458-855-6.
- The Scientific Basis of Oral Health Education (BDJ Books), Levine and Stillman-Lowe. 0-904588-84-x.
- The Skilled Helper (Brooks Cole), G Egan. 13-978049560413.
- Train your Team yourself (How to Books), Lisa Hadfield-Law. 1-85703-741-3.
- Understanding Body Language (Hodder Stoughton), Ribbens and Thompson. 0-340-78176-9.
- Who Killed Change (Harper Collins Publishers), Ken Blanchard. 978-0-00-731749-3.
- Zapp the Power of Enlightenment (Century Business), Byham and Cox. 0-09-174922-0.

Glossary

Accident	The HSE define an accident as "any unplanned event that resulted in injury or ill health of people, or damage or loss to property, plant, materials or the environment or a loss of business opportunity"
Adjourning	Bruce Tuckman's fifth stage of team formation
Assets	What a business owns
Balance sheet	In financial accounting, a balance sheet or statement of financial position is a summary of the financial balances of a sole proprietorship, a business partnership or a company. Assets, liabilities and ownership equity are listed as of a specific date, such as the end of its financial year
Break even	The point at which income matches expenditure
Bruce Tuckman	Bruce Wayne Tuckman born 1938 – an American psychologist who carried our research to establish a theory of group dynamics
Business strategy	A term used in business planning that implies a careful selection and application of resources to obtain predetermined objectives
Capital expenditure	The net invoice price of equipment, including the cost of any modifications, attachments, accessories, or auxiliary apparatus necessary to make it usable
Cash flow gap	The difference between income and expenditure
Cash flow statement	A financial report that shows incoming and outgoing money during a particular period (often monthly or quarterly). It does not include non-cash items such as depreciation. This makes it useful for determining the short-term viability of a company, particularly its ability to pay bills
Cash Inflow	Money earned and received by the company
Cash outflow	Money spent by the business in order to trade
Communication chain	Interlinked activities aiming to pass information from one person to others
Continuing Professional Development	Ongoing development of work related knowledge and skills

Dental Practice Management

Contract of employment	An legal agreement between employer and employee
COSHH	Control of Substances Hazardous to Health as define in Health and Safety law
Cost of sales	Costs directly related to the purchase or production of what the company sells
County Court	The judicial body of the civil justice system in England and Wales
Critical analysis	A purposeful and reflective analysis leading to judgment of the value of the results of a project
Crown Court	The judicial body of the criminal justice system in England and Wales
Deming's 14 points	William Edwards Deming (14 October 1900 – 20 December 1993) was an American statistician, professor, author, lecturer, and consultant. Deming's business philosophy is summarised in his famous "14 Points," listed below. These points have inspired significant changes among a number of companies striving to compete in the world's increasingly competitive environment.
Disciplinary and grievance procedures	Procedures set out in employment law for resolving disputes between employers and employees
Discrimination	To treat someone less favourably based on a 'protected characteristic'
Duty of care	The obligation that a person has to exercise reasonable care with respect to the interests of others, including protecting them from harm
EU	The European Union (EU) is an economic and political union of member states, located primarily in Europe. Committed to regional integration, the EU was established by the Treaty of Maastricht on 1 November 1993 upon the foundations of the European Community
Elements of administration	"Functions" of the administrator as described by Henri Fayol as "the 5 elements of administration"
Employment Tribunals	Employment Tribunals are independent judicial bodies who determine disputes between employers and employees over employment rights

Equality Act 2010	The Equality Act 2010 brings disability, sex, race and other grounds of discrimination within one piece of legislation, and made changes to the law
European Court of Justice (ECJ)	Court of Justice of the European Communities. The Court is responsible for settling disputes relating to European Community Law
European Directives	A Directive is a legislative act of the European Union, which requires member states to achieve a particular result without dictating the means of achieving that result
External customer	Customers who purchase goods or services from a provider (business)
Fair dismissal	Termination of employment using permitted procedures under permissible circumstances
Fixed overheads	Costs associated with businesses activities incurred irrespective of levels of sales made
Forming	Bruce Wayne Tuckman's first stage of team formation
Freedom of Information Act 2000	An Act of the Parliament of the UK, it is the implementation of freedom of information legislation and introduces a public "right to know" in relation to public bodies
Gantt Chart	A type of bar chart that illustrates a project schedule. Gantt charts illustrate the start and finish dates of the terminal elements and summary elements of a project. Terminal elements and summary elements comprise the work breakdown structure of the projec.
General Dental Council	The General Dental Council was created under the Dentist Act to 'Regulate the Dental Team and Protect the General Public'
Gestalt	A term used to describe circumstances in which the whole is different from the sum of its parts
Harassment	Unwanted conduct which is considered by the recipient be unreasonable or offensive
Hazard	Any source of potential damage, harm or adverse health effects on something or someone under certain conditions at work
Health and Safety At Work Act 1974	Lays down minimum standards for health and safety in the workplace

Dental Practice Management

Health and Social Care Act 2008	Set up the Care Quality Commission (CQC) as regulator of health and adult social care in England, they make sure that the care people receive meets essential standards of quality and safety and encourage ongoing improvements by those who provide or commission care. In addition to the assurance about compliance with essential standards the CQC provides independent, reliable and timely information about the quality of care in providers above essential standards, and about the quality of care secured by commissioners for their local communities
Health and Safety Management	Occupational health and safety is a cross-disciplinary area concerned with protecting the safety, health and welfare of people engaged in work or employment
Henri Fayol	Henri Fayol (Istanbul, 29 July 1841 – Paris, 19 November 1925) was a French mining engineer, director of mines, and management theorist, who developed independent of the theory of Scientific Management, a general theory of business administration
Improvement Notices	Improvement notices are one of a range of means which enforcing authorities use to achieve the broad aim of dealing with serious risks, securing compliance with Health and Safety law and preventing harm. An Improvement Notice allows time for the recipient to comply
Induction procedure	An organised process to introduce new employees to the culture and processes of their workplace
Internal customer	Internal customer is a technical term used in management science popularised by Joseph M. Juran
Job description	An outline of the duties, responsibilities and reporting structure of the workplace
Kaizen	*Kaizen* (Japanese for "improvement" or "change for the better") refers to a philosophy or practices that focus upon continuous improvement of processes and procedures
Key Performance Indicators	A quantifiable measurement that can be used to track the progress in achieving important goals within a company
Level 4 Qualifications	First degree level qualifications for operational managers

Level 5 Qualifications	Higher degree level qualifications for strategic managers
Liabilities	An amount of money in a company that is owed to someone and has to be paid in the future, such as tax, debt, interest, and mortgage payments
Macro market	Refers to a marketer's effort to reach a broader target group via a specific campaign. This is often researched through the application of a PESTLE Analysis
Management accounts	Usually comprise the profit and loss account and balance sheet, but there is no rule as to what financial information is presented, or how, as these accounts are for internal use only, to assist the company directors with managing the business. Usually prepared monthly
Management models	The process of generating methods, techniques and theories. A scientific model can provide a way to read elements and predict outcomes
Management science	The application of scientific methods and principles to management decision making and problem solving. Management science encompasses the use of quantitative, mathematical, and statistical techniques. The term can be used to denote scientific management, which has origins in the work of Frederick Winslow Taylor and Henry Gantt.
Marketing Mix	The term "marketing mix" was coined in 1953 by Neil Borden and describes the role of the marketing manager as a "mixer of ingredients", who sometimes follows recipes prepared by others, sometimes prepares his own recipe as he goes along, sometimes adapts a recipe from immediately available ingredients, and at other times invents new ingredients no one else has tried
Micro market	Market conditions that exist within the business, such as, the skills and aptitudes needs and expectation of the work team, often researched using the Marketing Mix
Near Miss Incident	A "near-miss" incident can be defined as, "any event, which under slightly different circumstances, may have resulted in injury or ill health of people, or damage or loss to property, plant, materials or the environment or a loss of business opportunity".

Dental Practice Management

Net profit	The profit made by a business after the cost of sales has been deducted
Norming	Bruce Tuckman's third stage of team formation
Notes to the accounts	These form part of the annual financial statements of a company. They supply more information on the figures contained in the financial accounts
Operating profit	In accounting, profit is the difference between price and the costs of bringing to market
Operational management process	An area of business concerned with the production of goods and services, which involves the responsibility of ensuring that business operations are efficient in terms of using as little resource as needed, and effective in terms of meeting customer requirements
Over heads	In business, overhead, overhead cost or overhead expense refers to an ongoing expense of operating a business (also known as Operating expenses - rent, gas/electricity, wages etc).
PDCA Cycle	DCA (plan-do-check-act) is an iterative four-step problem-solving process typically used in business process improvement. It is also known as the Deming cycle, Shewhart cycle, Deming wheel, or plan-do-study-act
Parato analysis	Pareto analysis is a statistical technique in decision making that is used for selection of a limited number of tasks that produce significant overall effect. It uses the Pareto principle - the idea that by doing 20% of work you can generate 80% of the advantage of doing the entire job
Performance appraisal	A performance appraisal, employee appraisal, performance review, or (career) development discussion is a method by which the job performance of an employee is evaluated (generally in terms of quality, quantity, cost, and time) typically by their manager or supervisor
Performing	Bruce Tuckman's fourth stage of team formation
Person centred systems	The development of systems and processes that meet the needs of both internal and external customers
Pestle analysis	A recognised technique for examining features of the business environment

Policy	An agreed reaction to specified circumstances, pre-agreed by the business in line with its business plan, philosophy and objectives
PPE	Personal Protective Equipment use for Health and Safety purposes
Practice philosophy	The guiding principles used by the practice to guide decision making
Proactive management	Management by objective, in which goals are set and actions to secure these goals are determined and monitored
Procedure	An agreed course of action, set in policy to secure an agreed objective
Product benefits	The benefits of a product are what customer gains by purchasing it. For example the benefit of implant may be that the patient can eat more comfortably than they could with dentures
Product features	The features of a produce are aspects like cost, appearance, quality
Profit and Loss accounts	Is a review of the income and expenditure activities of the company over a given period of time
Projected income	A calculation of income, based on a systematic review of current market conditions
Protocol	Accepted ways of communication between work colleagues, developed to promote the culture of the workplace
Quality audit	A technique of TQM aiming to quality the product of a system or process
Reactive management	Management in response to events, sometimes called fire fighting
Remedial feedback	Feedback delivered during an appraisal intended to remedy unsatisfactory performance
Return on investment	(ROI) A calculation of the potential income from an input of time, money or resources
Revenue expenditure	Money spent on the day to day running of the business, for the settlement of the costs related to materials, premises, and staff wages
Risk assessment	A systematic assessment of work activities and premises with a view to identify hazards and manage the associated risks

Dental Practice Management

Robens Committee	Was formed to review the law related to workplace safety. The result was The Health and Safety at Work etc Act (1974), the Act, under which all UK safety legislation is consolidated. The HSAWA is an 'enabling' Act, which provides a framework under which legislation can be introduced to cover specific areas, e.g., COSHH, although there are few regulations within the Act itself. The Act covers anyone affected by work activities and brought 5 million workers not covered by the existing legislation under its protection
Small business	A company that employs fewer than 100 people and is usually a privately owned. Small businesses fuel local economic growth and innovation
SMART Objectives	Detailed analysis of business objectives to enable the manager to set qualitative and quantative measures to assess the results achieved
Statistical control of systems	A measure of how a system is performing based on the Edward-Deming approach to statistical measures of effectiveness and efficiency
Statement of commitment to Health and Safety	Employers are required to issue a statement of how they plan to meet health and safety requirements
Storming	Tuckman's second stage of team formation
Strategic policy	A major part of the management process, which is concerned with defining ends, means and conduct at every level of the organisation
SWOT Analysis	A systematic way to analyse the strengths, weaknesses of the internal condition and , opportunities and threats of external conditions
Training Needs Analysis	A rational approach to assessing the training needs or development needs of employees
Tom Peters	In conjunction with Bob Waterman identified 'Eight Attributes of Excellence'
Total Quality Management	Total Quality Management focuses upon customer-supplier relationship (external and internal customers and suppliers) and the systems used
Variable costs/	The cost of materials or overheads that change according to how

Overheads   much work is done
Victimisation   To treat someone less favourably, unfairly, to single someone out
                  for punishment or make them a victim

Index

80-20 Rule	8	Care Quality Standards(England)	46
		Cash flow - cycle	64
A		Cash flow - forecast	65
Aims and Objectives	13	Cash Flow - management	64
Adjourning	81	Cash Flow - projection	58
Appointment Book	67	Cash Flow - statement	18, 61
Appraisals	76, 78, 84, 86, 90	Clinical Governance	9, 44
Appraisals - Case study	87	Communication - Chain	79
Arbitration and Conciliation Advisory		Communication	33
Service - ACAS	98	Communication -channels	79
Audit	24, 40	Complaints	32
Audit and Review	120	Conduct	101

Continuous Professional
Development   32, 74, 76, 90

B

Balance Sheet	18, 61	Continuous Professional	
BDA Good Practice scheme	45,48	Development- evidence	93
Benchmarking	37,59	Continuous Professional	
Best Practice	44,	Development - general	81
Breakeven	64	Continuous Professional	
British Chambers of Commerce	2	Development - planning	76
Budgets	60	Continuous Professional	
Budget -Management	65	Development - records	76
Budgetary- Targets	69	Continuous Professional	
Bullying	101,105	Development -verifiable	74
Business Goals	14	Continuous Improvement	50
Business Plan	13,22,58,68,78	Cost of Sales	29
Business Planning -long,		Costs - variable , fixed	65
middle, short term	66	Courts System	96, 97
		Critical Analysis	22, 40
C		Customer Care Strategy	36
Capability/performance	101	Customer Feedback	31
Capital Expenditure	65		
Care Quality Commission	5, 7, 43,	**D**	
	45, 58, 70, 81, 88,111	Dental Care Professionals	48

Dentists Act	44	Forming	65

G

Design	74		
Disciplinary - interviews	24	General Dental Council	31, 32, 74,
Discrimination, direct	102, 107	Grievance and Disciplinary Procedures	90
Discrimination, indirect	108	Gross misconduct	100, 104
Discrimination, by Perception	108		
Dismissal	109		
Duty of Care	104		

H

Harassment	101
Health and safety	114, 119, 121
Health and Safety at Work Act 1974	127
Health and Safety - COSHH	114, 121
Health and Safety- Domino Theory	116
Health and Safety - enforcement	117
Health and Safety - Executive	124
Health and Safety - Improvement Notice	116
Health and Safety - Inspectors	116
Health and Safety - management	116
Health and Safety - policy statement	105, 108
Health and Safety - prevention	96
Health and Safety - policy distribution	114, 128
Health and Safety - Prohibition Notice	119
Health and Safety - Prosecution	117
Health and Safety - reporting RIDDOR	126
Health and Safety - Six Pack 1992	127
Health and Social Care Act	117
Hourly rate	43, 44

E

Effective	115, 126
Efficient	50
Emotional Intelligence	50
Employees Rights	97, 111
Employment Contracts	130
Employment Relations Directorate	98
Employment Tribunals	96
Equal Pay	96, 111
Equality Act 2010	96
Equality and Human Rights	105, 107
Essential Standards of Quality and Safety	96
European Directives	44, 96
Evaluation	115
Evidence based decisions	24, 41
External Customers	60

F

Financial - governance	60
Financial - targets	58, 71
Financial - performance	60
Financial - record keeping	60
Financial - results	63
Financial - terminology	68
Financial - plan	32
Five Forces of Competitive Position	58
Fixed Costs	28, 65

I

Implementation	67
In-house - complaints scheme	24
In-house - training	33
Induction	83, 91,

Dental Practice Management

Induction Case Study 90
Informed Consent 78, 83
Internal Customers 45
Interview Techniques 31
Initiation 87

J

Job Descriptions 24, 78, 81

K

Kaizen 90
Key Performance Indicators 44

M

Management - Accounts 58
Management Models 62
Management Models - Cooperative Model 12
Management Models - Team Management Model 12
Management Roles 12
Management Science 5, 8
Management Techniques- Gantt Chart 6, 37
Management Techniques - Mind Mapping- Buzan 9
Management Techniques - PEST (LE) Analysis 6, 22, 25, 68
Management Techniques - Planning 6
Management Techniques - SMART Objectives 9, 24, 29, 35, 37, 40
Management Techniques - SWOT analysis 6, 22, 28, 29, 33, 68
Management Techniques - Pareto Analysis 8
Management Theories - Deming's 14 Points 4

Management Theories - Drucker Peter, 3, 9, 24
Management Theories Farol Henri - Elements of Administration 3, 9, 24
Management Theories - Peters Tom 3
Management Theories - Porter Michael 28
Management Theories - Tuckman B 81
Marketing Techniques 22
Market Research 23
Marketing - call for action 39
Marketing - e-marketing 11
Marketing - features and benefits 29
Marketing mix 29
Marketing - definition of 22
Marketing - macro market 23, 26
Marketing - micro market 23, 28
Measuring Performance 5
Mentoring 90

N

National Qualifications and Curriculum Authority 18
Norming 81
Notes to the Accounts 60, 62

O

Objectives 22, 24, 60, 62
Operating Expenses 58
Operating profit 61
Operational Management Process 18
Overheads 59

P

PDCA Cycle 50
Peer Review 92
Performance Analysis- Financial 69
Performance Reviews 84

Performing	81
Personal Development Plan (PDP)	75, 90
Personnel Management	73
Personnel Records	85
Policy, Process and Procedure	53, 78
Policy Building	54
Postgraduate Training	92
Practice Rules	106
Pricing services	67
Professional Associations	92
Profit and Loss Account	11, 61
Protected Characteristics	108
Purchasers and Providers	35

Q

Quality Audit	50
Quality Cycle	50
Quality Management	22, 43
Quality Management - Crosby PB	49
Quality Management - Deming	44, 46
Quality Management - Feigenbaum	49
Quality Management - Juran	48
Quality Management - Peters	49
Quality Management - Shewhart	48
Quality Theorists - Taugi	49
Questionnaires	37
QUITE- Quality Focus	56

R

Rate of Return(ROR)	5
Recipe for Quality	47
Reflective Practice	76
Registered Manager	24
Research	3, 23
Return on Investment (ROI)	2, 5, 38
Revenue	61

Revenue Expenditure	65
Risk Assessment	114, 127
Robens Committee	114
Role of Practice Manager	56

S

Service Standards	37
Small Business	14
Staff Development	41
Staff Handbook	100
Standards for Dental Professionals	37, 74
Stock Levels	59
Storming	81

T

Tactics	53
Targets	36
Team Debriefs	76
Team Development	74
Team Development- systems	78
The 3 C's Technique	32
Training and Development Policy	88
Treatment Coordination	36
Trust	88

V

Variable costs	65
Victimisation	109

W

Warnings	103
Whole Team Professionalism	44
Workplace Stress	128